Equity, Diversity and Inclusion Explained

Equity, Diversity and Inclusion Explained

Shakil Butt

KoganPage

Publisher's note

Every possible effort has been made to ensure that the information contained in this book is accurate at the time of going to press, and the publishers and authors cannot accept responsibility for any errors or omissions, however caused. No responsibility for loss or damage occasioned to any person acting, or refraining from action, as a result of the material in this publication can be accepted by the editor, the publisher or the author.

First published in Great Britain and the United States in 2025 by Kogan Page Limited

Kogan Page

Kogan Page Ltd, 2nd Floor, 45 Gee Street, London EC1V 3RS, United Kingdom
Kogan Page Inc, 8 W 38th Street, Suite 902, New York, NY 10018, USA
www.koganpage.com

EU Representative (GPSR)

Authorised Rep Compliance Ltd, Ground Floor, 71 Baggot Street Lower, Dublin D02 P593, Ireland
www.arccompliance.com

Kogan Page books are printed on paper from sustainable forests.

© Kogan Page, 2025

ISBNs

Hardback	978 1 3986 2453 5
Paperback	978 1 3986 2454 2
Ebook	978 1 3986 2455 9

British Library Cataloguing-in-Publication Data

A CIP record for this book is available from the British Library.

Typeset by Hong Kong FIVE Workshop, Hong Kong
Printed and bound by CPI Group (UK) Ltd, Croydon CR0 4YY

Contents

Introduction

Introducing this book

This book has been written for the early-career Human Resources (HR) professional who is either tasked with Equality, Diversity and Inclusion (EDI) or wanting to embed EDI in every aspect of your HR work. You may be undertaking your first role in HR or be in the early stages of your HR career.

This book aims to provide a grounding in the evolving world of EDI, from the 1900s to the present day. It seeks to introduce concepts such as discrimination and bias, and encourage you to consider your own perceptions and biases as part of this process. It aims to provide evidence and research on EDI, while also offering practical advice on how to recognize discrimination and implement EDI initiatives to address it within your organization. Throughout, you will find boxed contributions from experts in the EDI field to give more detail and insight into key points.

Understanding how EDI has evolved, the legislation that has been passed to tackle discrimination and relevant legal cases and tribunals will help to elevate you as a knowledgeable EDI champion and trusted partner. It will also help you to offer evidence-based advice on all matters related to EDI.

Throughout the book, you will find a range of reflection points, tips and exercises. Many chapters include 'What would you do?' exercises, which encourage you to think through how you could act in scenarios you are likely to encounter in your role. The Appendix includes suggested responses to these exercises. Each chapter also has review questions to test your learning and understanding. Use the endnotes to find out more about the research that's discussed throughout.

The reflection points, review questions and exercises included throughout the chapters are designed to deepen your learning and set the discussion in your unique organizational context.

If you are not currently in an EDI role but aspire to be, there is plenty for you in this book, too. When you come to a reflection exercise or activity, you can think about this from a hypothetical perspective.

The concluding chapter provides further guidance on how you can assess your current skills, as well as some top tips and recommendations for action, all helping you to continue to learn about EDI.

An overview of Equity, Diversity and Inclusion

If you have been given EDI as part of your remit in HR, you are likely to have heard of the acronym. You may also be familiar with other acronyms which more or less amount to the same thing, but you may be unsure of the difference. EDI (Equality or Equity, Diversity and Inclusion) is sometimes rearranged and listed as DEI. It also has variations sometimes combined with other letters, most notably being EDIB, where 'B' is Belonging. Others include:

- JEDI (Justice, Equality, Diversity and Inclusion)
- IDEA (Inclusion, Diversity, Equity and Accessibility)
- DICE (Diversity, Inclusion, Culture and Ethics)
- DIB (Diversity, Inclusion and Belonging)
- DEIB (Diversity, Equality, Inclusion and Belonging)
- DEIBA (Diversity, Equality, Inclusion, Belonging and Accessibility)
- WEI (Wellbeing, Engagement and Inclusion)

Outside of EDI practitioners and some HR professionals, the terms Equity (or Equality), Diversity and Inclusion, are often used interchangeably as if they are one and the same. While they are interdependent and related, the three terms are distinct from one another.

Responsibility for EDI often sits with an EDI lead or someone in HR. That's probably why you're reading this book. Ideally, accountability should sit with everyone in the organization, from new hires at the start of their careers to senior leadership. Part of any EDI champion's role is to make this happen.

EDI isn't about designing and implementing expensive, showy initiatives. It's about creating a culture of inclusion, recognizing the lived experiences of an organization's employees and allowing diversity to belong.

The structure of this book

This book first considers EDI as a concept, how it fits within HR and why it is important and necessary. Chapter 1 kicks off by introducing EDI as a concept, the meaning behind the words 'equity', 'diversity' and 'inclusion' and looking at discrimination through the ages. Chapter 2 then considers HR's role in EDI and terms you will need to be familiar with as an early career HR practitioner working in this area. Chapters 3 and 4 show us how we all have biases and preconceptions that can lead to unhelpful and impaired thinking. They emphasize the need for us to consider our potential biases and recognize how social conditioning may have led us to think the way we do, applying this to the point of view of EDI at work.

The book then moves on to EDI in organizations. Chapter 5 looks at practical EDI initiatives that many organizations implement. It considers how many organizations focus on 'best practice', when it would be better to focus on 'best fit'. Chapter

6 looks at talent, and the importance of carefully considering how to attract, develop and remunerate diverse talent. In Chapter 7, we look at how discrimination shows up in the workplace, so you know what to look out for, and in Chapter 8, we look at how to gain buy-in for EDI initiatives and build a business case.

Finally, the Conclusion provides the opportunity to reflect on your current skills and create an action plan for implementing an effective EDI strategy.

CHAPTER ONE

Introducing equity, diversity and inclusion

Introduction

This chapter begins by explaining the meaning behind the terms 'equity', 'diversity' and 'inclusion', paying particular attention to the difference between equity and equality. We also consider 'belonging' as a related concept, and something that is often added to the acronym, EDI to form EDIB.

Next, we consider the importance of attracting diverse talent to your organization to put you at a competitive advantage. Having people at all levels of the organization who reflect your customers will allow you to develop products and services that resonate with your target market.

We look at how the modern world of work has evolved, and the insight that gives us into understanding why EDI is so hard. We end the chapter by looking at the history of discrimination in the UK since the 1900s, and legislation that has been introduced to try and address it. We pay particular attention to the Equality Act 2010, as this is what you will need to be most aware of in your capacity as an early career HR professional working in EDI.

By the end of this chapter, you will have a good understanding of what EDI means, how it relates to organizations and why it is so very important to get it right.

LEARNING OBJECTIVES

By the end of this chapter, you will be able to:

- Understand key terms: (E) Equality or Equity, (D) Diversity and (I) Inclusion.
- Assess disparity in the workplace and missed opportunities.
- Appreciate why EDI is an uphill challenge.
- Describe equality and discrimination legislation since the 1900s, and explain important aspects of the Equality Act 2010.
- Appreciate the context of political and world events and how these influence attitudes towards equality and marginalized groups.

Equality and equity

Equality is defined by the Collins Dictionary as 'the same status, rights and responsibilities for all the members of a society, group, or family'.[1]

Equality is a fairly well-embedded term in the workplace. This isn't because it is the most apt, but because of the strapline, 'we are an equal opportunity employer', often found in job adverts. The strapline itself is linked to the prominence and importance of the Equality Act 2010, a critical piece of legislation that has a huge impact on society. We cover it in detail later in this chapter.

The aspiration to treat everyone equally is a noble one, but this does necessarily ensure everyone is treated fairly. We are all different and, as such, have different needs.

Equity is a more appropriate term because it recognizes this and the need for fairness. The maturity of EDI in an organization determines which term is being more widely used.

EXPERT OPINION

Jenny Garrett, author of *Equality vs Equity*

Equity isn't synonymous with equality. While companies that strive for workplace equality aim to treat everyone the same without discrimination, they may overlook the need for equity. This means that the entire workforce falls under the same set of rules, privileges and employee experience design, without considering unique, demographic-related needs. Such an approach can inadvertently lead to an unfair work environment.

Equity, on the other hand, is about giving those from minoritized groups what they need to achieve equal outcomes. This involves recognizing and addressing the systems that disadvantage some individuals and seeking to overcome these barriers. Achieving equity requires an individual approach, focusing on leading, sharing power and prioritizing outcomes.

Treating everyone the same fails to recognize that everyone is uniquely human and has differing needs. For example, someone with caring responsibilities might value flexibility in their working hours, whereas someone else may prefer fixed traditional hours.

EXAMPLE

The following scenario can help to understand equality versus equity.

Three people – a child, an adult and a wheelchair user – are all given the same adult bike to ride. This is an example of equality, as everyone is being treated equally.

However, the child cannot reach the pedals, and the bike is not accessible for the wheelchair user. Giving the child an age-

appropriate bike and the wheelchair user an adapted bike treats
them according to their needs, making the solution more
equitable and cost-effective.

STOP AND THINK

Are your policies equitable? Policies are often applied with the
intent of treating everyone the same without considering what
would be more effective. This can be down to apathy, as creating
policies and processes designed to mirror individual needs
requires more effort, but it is likely to be far more impactful.

Diversity

Diversity is defined by Merriam-Webster as 'the condition of
having or being composed of differing elements'.[2] Kevin Green,
Chief People Officer at First Bus, explains in his book,
Competitive People Strategy that 'teams by their very nature are
made up of different people with different personalities, views,
opinions and perspectives. This diversity helps devise and deliver
solutions and enables progress to take place'.

EXPERT OPINION

Simon Fanshawe OBE, Co-Founder of Stonewall, Partner at Diversity
by Design and author of *The Power of Difference*

Done effectively, work on diversity and inclusion can deliver real
benefits to your company by:

- Understanding in detail and then removing blocks to talent –
  the diversity deficits – whether they impact on individuals or
  groups.

- Combining the difference each of your staff and colleagues
  bring to the business in the right way to produce a diversity
  dividend.

Diversity must be the starting point for organizations, but many struggle to reflect the community they are based in, and the customers or society they are reaching through their products and services. Increasingly, in a post-pandemic world, most organizations have national or international ambitions, which should stress the importance of reflecting that diversity internally, so they can understand their market and stakeholders.

In our personal lives, we encounter many situations where we expect to be able to make a decision based on a diverse range of options:

- Streaming platforms have a range of genres, films and shows.
- Restaurant menus have multiple options for starters, mains, desserts and drinks.
- Supermarkets have numerous product lines for every type of item, e.g. strawberry yoghurt comes in many varieties: low fat, creamy, smooth, thick, protein-rich etc.
- Car dealerships offer a range of makes, models, colours, used, new, manual, automatic, hybrid, saloon, hatchback and mileage for customers to select from.
- Estate agents list properties detailing type: detached or terraced, location, schools, amenities, parking, the neighbourhood etc.
- Relationships with spouses and partners will be based on various attributes and qualities.

The part of the brain that is accustomed to dealing with diversity in our personal lives gets dialled down in the workplace, leaving us feeling more comfortable with people like ourselves.

In the workplace, diversity efforts are often focused on protected characteristics, but real diversity encompasses much more.

> **Protected characteristics:** Characteristics belonging to people which are protected in law. In the UK, there are nine protected characteristics:

1 Age

2 Disability

3 Gender reassignment

4 Marriage and civil partnership

5 Pregnancy and maternity

6 Race

7 Religion or philosophical belief

8 Sex

9 Sexual orientation

We often become aware of these differences in the school playground, and they become the basis of ridicule and/or isolation. These can include the following:

- Body shape, whether being tall or short, small or large.
- Facial features, which can be anything from nose to ear shape.
- Regional differences, including accents.
- Hair length, colour and/or style.
- Social class.

The truth is, no two people are alike. Even identical twins have different personalities and habits. There is a famous quote, 'If everyone is thinking alike, then somebody isn't thinking'. It's often attributed to General George S. Patton, who played a big part in World War II. Whether he said it or not, the sentiment goes to the heart of diversity. If everyone is thinking the same way, you're going to miss out on independent thought. As human beings with different lived experiences, we should all feel able to bring our differing perspectives and contributions to any issue, rather than parroting what someone else has put forward. A lack of difference stifles debate, hampers innovation and causes the status quo to go unchallenged.

> **KEY POINT**
>
> Being different makes us uniquely human, so we should celebrate that difference rather than fixating on it in an unproductive manner. We should be able to agree to disagree without being disagreeable.

Inclusion

If diversity is the starting point, then inclusion really is the next mountain peak. Inclusion is defined by the Cambridge Dictionary as the 'act of including someone or something as part of a group'.[3]

> **EXPERT OPINION**
> **Stephen Frost, CEO of Included and author of** *The Key to Inclusion*
>
> Inclusion is a noun – it's a state of incorporating others into groups or resources. The spirit of inclusion is also a verb, a call to action, to make sure people are accounted for.
>
> Inclusion is perhaps most easily understood by the counterfactual – many of us can relate to being excluded – left out, passed over, forgotten. Inclusion is making amends for this. If we don't consciously include, we may unconsciously exclude.
>
> Finally, inclusion is not necessarily about being charitable. While it can be, it's more about reaping the benefits of difference, for all concerned.

David Liddle, Founder of TCM and author of *Transformational Culture*, describes an inclusive workplace as one 'where we can be the best version of ourselves, free from others judging, condemning or excluding people because of their differences'. He suggests that in an inclusive workplace 'differences are a sign of strength, not a cause of adversity; where each voice is heard and each contribution is valued'.[4]

To really understand inclusion, it is probably better to reflect on exclusion. At some point in our lives, we have faced exclusion. The following scenarios are all examples of exclusion:

- A first day at school where everyone has made friends, and you have not 'clicked with the cool kids'.
- A new job and everyone already knows everyone else. They share banter that you can't join with.
- A group of friends went on a night out but didn't invite you and they are now reminiscing about what 'so and so' got up to.
- A WhatsApp group that you are not a part of. It's been going for a while, but no one thought to add you.

We all know how those moments feel. It is emotionally painful. In fact, it is more than that.

Amy Brann, a leading expert in applied neuroscience, has done extensive research on this phenomenon. MRI scans reveal that the same parts of the brain that register exclusion also react to physical pain. In other words, this pain is very real to the person experiencing it.[5]

REAL-WORLD EXAMPLE
Mrs S Hamilton versus Epsom and St Helier University Hospitals
NHS Trust[6]

An NHS nurse, Susan Hamilton, who was excluded by a colleague, won her claim of unfair constructive dismissal at an employment tribunal. Hamilton resigned in January 2022 from Epsom and St Helier University Hospitals NHS Trust.

She claimed that a co-worker showed 'bullying behaviour' towards her. He had ignored her in meetings, and 'stopped making tea for her when he was making it for all other team members'.

Hamilton was awarded £41,000, as a consequence of poor management by her employer.

In the workplace, a lack of inclusion can lead to poor employee engagement. At best, it can impact productivity, and at worst, result in high staff turnover, negating the hard work done to attract diversity in the first place.

True inclusion should feel like an all-inclusive resort, where breakfast, lunch, dinner, snacks, drinks, the beach, the pool, the activities, the gym etc. are all included. Nothing is off limits. That is what inclusion should feel like for someone from a diverse background. Nothing is off limits; everything is available; real equal opportunity.

A common phrase used by EDI practitioners is 'diversity is being invited to the party. Inclusion is being asked to dance'. It is a great expression, but it falls short. Real inclusion is 'choosing the song to dance to'.

> **KEY POINT**
>
> Inclusion in the workplace is being able to influence and shape the decisions and policies that impact the person who is different, rather than simply being on the receiving end of those decisions.

Belonging

> **EXPERT OPINION**
> Nicholé McGill-Higgins, Founder and Director, BEE-Longing
>
> Bee-Longing is not just a feeling – it's a framework I created, built on Belonging, Empathy and Equity. Belonging isn't about fitting in; it's about knowing who you are and being valued without conditions. People can't truly belong somewhere if they don't first belong to themselves. That's where empathy and equity come in – empathy ensures people are recognized, respected and understood for who they are, and equity ensures they have what they need to thrive. Without them, inclusion is performative. With them,

> belonging becomes the foundation of a culture where people – and organizations – flourish.

Belonging is often added to the acronym EDI, creating EDIB. Belonging is that sense of human connection that comes from being included. Often, belonging is measured through several staff survey questions, such as:

- 'I would recommend this place to others as a good place to work.'
- 'My opinions are valued at work.'
- 'I feel respected by my colleagues and leaders.'
- 'I can be my authentic self at work.'
- 'I feel aligned with the organization's mission and values.'
- 'I feel a strong sense of belonging at this organization.'
- 'The people I work with care about me as a person.'
- 'The organization creates an environment where I feel included.'
- 'I trust my coworkers and leaders to support me when I need it.'
- 'I feel like I can grow and succeed in my career here.'

EXERCISE

Does your organization run a staff survey, and if so, does it include questions to assess the level of belonging among employees? Are there any examples of how the results of these questions have led to action to address shortcomings? Do some research and/or ask your colleagues if you are not sure of the answer.

BELONGING AND MASLOW'S HIERARCHY OF NEEDS

Abraham Maslow was a psychologist who suggested that, as human beings, we have a hierarchy of needs.[7] These needs start with basic physiological needs and progress through safety, social, esteem needs until self-actualization needs are reached at the top of the hierarchy. Needs higher up the hierarchy cannot be pursued until the needs lower down the hierarchy are met.

Safety is the second need from the bottom of the hierarchy after physiological needs. This highlights the feeling of safety as an important human need. In the workplace, if a diverse person does not feel safe due to discriminatory behaviours, they are more likely to withdraw, which can lead to high staff turnover.

The next need – social – encompasses feelings of belonging. If someone is feeling ostracized and alone, their work will suffer, impacting both quality and productivity. The workplace will become burdensome, which will, again, lead to high staff turnover.

The absence of safety and belonging undermines self-esteem, the next need in the hierarchy. Self-esteem is replaced with self-doubt. Consequently, self-actualization, at the top of the hierarchy, (which means being the best version of yourself) is undermined, which leads to a lack of motivation and results in mediocrity.

That sense of ownership and affinity with the organization only happens once there is a feeling of safety and security in the role, and freedom to be your whole self, rather than conforming, looking over your shoulder, or searching for your next opportunity.

TIP

Belonging often surfaces in language. Get a sense of how strongly people feel they belong by listening to what they say:

- The organization becomes *my* organization.
- The team becomes *my* team.
- Objectives and work plans become *my* objectives and work plans.

Demographic disparity and talent shortages

When considering the statistical make-up of the UK, it is clear that large parts of society that could be employed are not reflected in the workplace. We will explore this through the lenses of gender, disability and race.

Gender disparity

Women are considered a minority in the workplace, and yet according to the Office for National Statistics 2023 census[8] in the UK, females account for 51 per cent of the population and 51 per cent of the working age population are also women.

According to the House of Commons Library 2024,[9] only 72.1 per cent of women aged 16 and over were employed, compared to 78.1 per cent male employment rate. This does not consider 38 per cent of women in employment working part-time, compared to 14 per cent of men.

According to the Government Equalities Office 2019,[10] mothers are more likely to withdraw from full-time employment after having children, compared to fathers. For those who do return to work, their career progression is often stunted, with a lower chance of receiving a promotion. Women's progression in the workplace continues to be held back by barriers, such as bias around pay and promotion, difficult workplace cultures (for example-sexual harassment), tensions between balancing work with care, and a shortage of quality part-time work with a good wage potential.

Disability disparity

The Office for National Statistics Census 2021,[11] across both England and Wales, reported that the proportion of disabled people, (whose day-to-day activities are limited by long-term physical or mental health conditions/illnesses) was 17.8 per cent. However, only about half of disabled people were in employment, compared to just over four in five non-disabled people. The employment gap was larger for disabled men than disabled women, with working disabled men more likely to be self-employed than non-disabled men. Working disabled people were also more likely to work part-time than non-disabled people.[12]

Race disparity

According to GOV.UK 2023, 30.2 million people of working age were from white ethnic groups and 7.2 per cent were Black/ Black African, 3.4 per cent were Indian, 2.7 per cent were Pakistani, with the remainder being mixed ethnicity and part of the 'other' ethnic group.[13]

Statista reported that in the UK during 2024, 8 per cent of Black working-age people were unemployed, compared to 10.2 per cent of Pakistanis and 5 per cent of Indians.[14]

The 'war for talent'

In Chapter 6, we consider the 'war for talent'[15] and the importance of attracting diverse talent to the workplace. Organizations that lack diverse talent put themselves at a competitive disadvantage.

For example, in 2023, McKinsey carried out research[16] on a number of companies and countries across six global regions and found that having more women represented on senior leadership teams meant organizations were 39 per cent more likely to financially outperform competitors who lacked diversity. Similarly, having more ethnic representation on senior leadership teams meant organizations were 39 per cent more likely to financially outperform its competitors, if they lacked diversity.

It's not rocket science. If the people at the helm reflect the people they are trying to reach, then the products and services are more likely to resonate with that target market. By bringing in directors with different backgrounds and unique insights that go beyond an organization's primary verticals, companies can take advantage of leadership that asks a different set of questions and offers a wider range of ideas, using uncommon approaches.

The argument behind the war for talent is to gain a competitive advantage in what are often saturated markets. To attract diverse talent, an employer needs to be an employer of choice, which is why organizations covet awards like UK's Best Workplaces[17] and dream about being recognized by Glassdoor,[18] in the hopes of building that employer brand.

> **STOP AND THINK**
>
> How diverse is your organization in regard to gender, ethnicity and disability?

Why is EDI so hard?

Getting EDI right is hard. To understand why, let's briefly consider how the modern world of work, as we understand it, was constructed.

It is almost impossible to study leadership and management without reference to some of the early pioneers of the 19th century, following the first and second industrial revolutions, which began the move away from home-based industries to wide-scale production.

During this period, Fredrick Wilmslow Taylor published, 'The Principles of Scientific Management' in 1911,[19] while Henri Fayol set out 14 principles of management in 1916.[20] The principles were adopted widely as businesses tried to raise revenues while lowering costs, in the pursuit of efficiency.

Simultaneously, Henry Ford's production lines and the introduction of the Ford Model T automobile in 1908 revolutionized transportation and the wider global industry.

These principles and practices were emulated by others, thereby creating the world of work as we know it today, with head offices, consumers and supplier chains used to yield profits or surpluses.

This world of work was imagined by white, straight, able-bodied men who envisioned work carried out by other white, straight, able-bodied men, as certainly, positions of authority were held by white, straight able-bodied men. There was no place for difference in this construct.

The first time women came into the workplace in the UK, in any substantial numbers, was during World War I, where they continued the work on farms and factories, while the men went off to fight. The war came to an end, and the women returned to their homes. The second time women came into the workplace in the UK, in any real numbers, was during World War II, this time to support the war effort more directly. The war came to an end, and the women again returned to their homes.

It was not until the NHS was established in 1948 that women entered the workplace in large numbers to stay. The challenge faced by women and minorities is explored further later in the chapter, when we look at discrimination through the ages, but the point being made is that from the outset, there was a distinct lack of diversity, which was by design and not by accident.

This is why it is so hard to tackle EDI in workplaces, as we are are pushing back against a legacy of discrimination that dates to the early 1900s. Change, while happening, is slow. Why? Some senior leaders see difference as a threat, worried they are being replaced by that difference, so they do not willingly want to give up power. But these leaders are missing the point. It is not about giving up power. It is about sharing that power to become even more powerful. Together, we are stronger. Discrimination, bias and how this shows up in the employee journey are all explored further in Chapters 3, 6 and 7, respectively. We'll end this chapter with a look at discrimination through the ages.

Discrimination through the ages

What happens in wider society directly affects the workplace, which has meant some strands of difference are ahead of others when it comes to awareness, understanding and support.

Political movements and social activism like #MeToo, #BLM and Stonewall have had greater success pushing aspects of EDI up the agenda of organizations. These movements have highlighted systemic inequalities and led to efforts by wider society to address discrimination, promote equity and create more inclusive environments, especially addressing particular protected characteristics.

Organizations usually focus on the Equality Act 2010, as it consolidated existing discrimination legislation, and gave more visibility and support to marginalized groups. Nevertheless, it is important to be aware of legislation and events prior to, and after the Equality Act 2010, to understand why it has been so difficult to address inequity. This section gives a whistlestop tour of equality and discrimination legislation in the UK since the 1900s. Use it as a quick reference guide to respond to queries in your organization about legislation and the social and political events that have led up to it. Knowing this history will help you cement your position as an EDI expert in your organization.

The Equality Act 2010 is one of the main reference points for both employer and employee in managing employee relations, but has it been a game changer? Consider this question as you work through this book.

1900s to 1969

THE SEX DISQUALIFICATION (REMOVAL) ACT 1919
Women were barred from professions such as law, civil service and academia; the Sex Disqualification (Removal) Act 1919 eliminated these restrictions.

THE DISABLED PERSONS ACT 1944

A quota system required employers with 20 or more employees to ensure at least 3 per cent of their workforce were people with a disability.

THE EDUCATION ACT 1944 (BUTLER ACT)

This act allowed women to access free secondary school education, previously denied, giving women access to greater employment opportunities.

The Act also declared mainstream schools as the most appropriate environment to teach disabled children, and ensured female teachers would not be forced to leave their jobs when they got married.

THE BRITISH NATIONALITY ACT 1948

After World War II, the British Nationality Act 1948, granted Commonwealth citizens the right to live and work in the UK, facilitating their migration in bringing their families with them to rebuild the nation.

1948 saw the arrival of 300,000 West Indians, known as the Windrush generation and named after the ship they arrived on. A further 300,000 people came from India, 140,000 from Pakistan and more than 170,000 from various parts of Africa.[21]

Racism and hostility against the migrants were widespread, and in the late 1950s, racial tensions led to rioting, notably in 1958, in Notting Hill and Nottingham, which was blamed on gangs of white youths.

Overseas in America, similar racial tensions led to the civil rights movement in 1955 following the lynching of Emmet Till, and Rosa Parks' arrest for refusing to give up her seat to a white passenger, which resulted in the Montgomery bus boycott.

THE RACE RELATIONS ACT 1965

Protests in 1963 took place against the Bristol bus company for refusing to employ Black and Asian people.[22] A boycott lasting four months led to the government initiating a first attempt to tackle discrimination on the 'grounds of colour, race, or ethnic or national origins' in public places, but this did not apply to jobs or housing. The Act also established the Race Relations Board and the National Committee for Commonwealth Immigrants.

THE SEXUAL OFFENCES ACT 1967

Male homosexuality was a criminal offence, dating back to the Middle Ages, with penalties including imprisonment, capital punishment or death. The Sexual Offences Act 1967 decriminalized homosexual acts between men over 21, provided they were consensual and conducted in private. The Act only applied to England and Wales, with gay sexual relations remaining illegal in Scotland and Northern Ireland until 1980 and 1982, respectively.

THE RACE RELATIONS ACT 1968

In 1967, the National Front, a far-right, fascist political party, was founded, stoking division and hatred, particularly against South Asian migrants.

The mood was captured in the scaremongering speech by British politician Enoch Powell, titled the 'Rivers of Blood', in which he warned of an impending clash.[23] Powell was critical of the rates of immigration from the Commonwealth to the United Kingdom, post-World War II.

The Race Relations Act 1968 expanded on the 1965 Act, preventing discrimination when it came to employment, housing and service provision, although this did not apply to the police force in its duties.

STONEWALL RIOTS 1969

Riots and demonstrations occurred in June 1969, in response to a police raid in New York at the Stonewall Inn, a gay club.[24] This mobilized the gay and lesbian community to push for change and greater acceptance. On the anniversary, peaceful demonstrations took place in American cities to commemorate the riots, which have since become an annual Pride celebration in June in major cities, globally.

1970s to 2009

THE EQUAL PAY ACT 1970

The act had been part of Labour's manifesto in 1964, brought into effect by strike action taken by female machinists at Ford Motor Company Limited's Dagenham plant in London. They decided to strike after being told their jobs were being graded Category C (less skilled, therefore less pay), while the men were being graded Category B (more skilled and therefore more pay).

The Equal Pay Act 1970[25] required women to be paid the same as men for performing the same or similar work, i.e. equal pay for equal work. To bring forward an equal pay claim, the claim needs to address the following three questions:

- Are the jobs comparable?
- If the jobs are comparable, are they of equal value?
- If they are of equal value, is there a reason why the roles should not be paid equally?

THE CHRONICALLY SICK AND DISABLED PERSONS ACT 1970

This was the first piece of global legislation to recognize and give rights to people with disabilities, introduced by Alf Morris MP, who went on to become the first Minister for the Disabled.

THE SEX DISCRIMINATION ACT 1975

The Sex Discrimination Act 1975 prohibited discrimination on the grounds of sex or marital status in employment, education and the provision of goods and services.

The Equal Opportunities Commission was established to prevent sex discrimination. Sex discrimination was now illegal unless employers had five or fewer people employed.

THE RACE RELATIONS ACT 1976

Building on previous race relations legislation, the Act extended protections against racial discrimination in employment, housing and public services, but this did not apply to the police.

The Race Relations Act 1976 made it illegal to discriminate against someone because of their race, colour, nationality, ethnic or national origin. The Commission for Racial Equality was established to address racial discrimination and promote racial equality.

RACE RIOTS 1981

Riots took place in Brixton, London, with clashes between the Black youth and the Metropolitan Police. Riots also took place in Handsworth, located in Birmingham, Toxteth, in Liverpool and Moss Side, in Manchester.

The riots in Brixton were in response to criticism over the handling of a police investigation, after 13 Black youths died in a house fire, and the police concluded it to have been accidental. The African-Caribbean community accused the police of disproportionately using 'stop and search' powers against Black people, which was upheld in the UK government's Scarman Report.[26]

THE DISABLED PERSONS ACT 1986

The Disabled Persons Act 1986 sought to improve services for people with disabilities, by strengthening their voice through representation and additional duties on local authorities.

STONEWALL ESTABLISHED 1989

Stonewall, named after the Stonewall riots, is a charity campaigning and advocating for LGBTQ+ rights.[27] Stonewall was established a year after Section 28 of the Local Government Act in 1988 was introduced, which prohibited the promotion of homosexuality by local authorities.

THE MAASTRICHT TREATY 1992

The UK, alongside other EU nations signed the Maastricht Treaty on European integration. This gave all EU citizens equal rights and freedom to live in any member state, allowing EU citizens, irrespective of which country they were from in the EU, to settle and work in a different EU country, leading to a surge in migrant workers. Other countries joined the EU in 2004: Cyprus, Czech Republic, Estonia, Latvia, Hungary, Lithuania, Malta, Poland, Slovakia and Slovenia.

STEPHEN LAWRENCE MURDER 1993

Stephen Lawrence was a Black, 18-year-old teenager murdered in a racially motivated attack by a group of six white youths, causing public outrage. The Metropolitan Police and the Criminal Prosecution Service were criticized over their handling of the murder investigation and the lack of prosecution.[28]

THE CRIMINAL JUSTICE AND PUBLIC ORDER ACT 1994

A failed amendment was put forward by Edwina Currie MP to lower the age of consent for homosexual acts, from 21 to 16, but did lead to the age of consent between two male partners being lowered to 18.

THE DISABILITY DISCRIMINATION ACT (DDA) 1995

Direct Action Network, an organization comprising disabled activists, was protesting over how they were portrayed as objects of pity by ITV during fundraising telethons.[29] Thousands of people took part handcuffing themselves to buses, blocking streets or demonstrating outside Parliament. Those arrested were released as the police did not have accessible vehicles to take them away, underscoring the issue with how disabled persons were not catered for.

The DDA 1995 made it illegal for employers and service providers to discriminate against someone disabled but fell short in a number of areas:

- 'Reasonable Adjustments' was introduced to remove barriers and create greater accessibility to services and opportunities, but this only applied to employers with more than 15 people, from 1996 onwards. Making buildings more accessible was not addressed until 2004.
- Reasonable adjustments were open to interpretation with greater expectations for larger, well-resourced organizations compared to smaller ones.
- There was no requirement for service providers to adjust their policies by making their documents accessible until 1999.
- Health conditions like cancer, HIV and multiple sclerosis were not covered from the point of being diagnosed, until 2005.
- There were no laws to prevent discriminating against disabled persons on transport or reasonable adjustments to housing until 2005.
- The Disability Rights Commission was established in 2000 to uphold the DDA 1995.

THE SEX DISCRIMINATION (GENDER REASSIGNMENT) REGULATIONS 1999

These regulations amended the Sex Discrimination Act 1975, allowing employment protection for people who had undergone or were proposing to undergo gender reassignment, i.e. those who are undergoing or have undergone a process changing from their biological sex to the opposite sex.

To be protected, there is no requirement for a trans person to have medical supervision or intervention, nor a Gender Recognition Certificate.

THE RACE RELATIONS (AMENDMENT) ACT 2000

A judicial inquiry occurred in 1993, commissioned by then Home Secretary, Jack Straw, into Stephen Lawrence's murder and subsequent investigation, chaired by Sir William

Macpherson. The Macpherson Report[30] found that many of the Scarman Report recommendations had been ignored and concluded that the Metropolitan Police was institutionally racist. To form the basis of the new Race Relations Act, 70 recommendations were made, bringing the police within scope of race relations legislation.

THE SEXUAL OFFENCES (AMENDMENT) ACT 2000
The Sexual Offences (Amendment) Act 2000 lowered the age of consent to 16 for same-sex couples in England, Scotland and Wales, and 17 in Northern Ireland.

THE SEXUAL OFFENCES ACT 2003
The Sexual Offences Act 2003 overrode the previous rules regarding privacy for gay men, allowing for public displays of homosexuality.

THE EMPLOYMENT EQUALITY (SEXUAL ORIENTATION AND RELIGION/ BELIEF) REGULATIONS 2003
The Employment Equality Regulations 2003 prohibited employers unreasonably discriminating against employees on grounds of sexual orientation, perceived sexual orientation, religion or belief:

- Sexual orientation is about who you are physically attracted to, whether this is the opposite gender, same gender or both.
- Religion referred to mainly world faiths with established beliefs, rituals and following.
- Philosophical belief needed to be genuinely held, serious and compatible with human dignity. Examples include environmentalism, anti-Zionism, veganism, pacifism, humanism and anti-fox hunting.

THE CIVIL PARTNERSHIPS ACT 2004
The Civil Partnerships Act gave similar rights and responsibilities to civil marriages. It was initially intended for same-sex

couples but changed in 2019 to include opposite-sex couples. The Act had provisions such as entitlement to the same property rights, the same exemptions regarding social security and pension benefits, as well as having the option to dissolve the partnership, similar to divorce.

THE DISABILITY DISCRIMINATION (AMENDMENT) ACT 2005

The 2005 Amendment to the DDA introduced a duty for public authorities to promote equality of opportunity for disabled people. It changed the definition of disability, so that it covered progressive conditions like cancer, HIV and multiple sclerosis from the point of diagnosis. Moreover, mental illnesses no longer needed to be 'clinically well-recognized' to be covered.

More emphasis was placed on service providers to make reasonable adjustments for disabled people and protection was extended to more employment categories, including police officers and partnerships.

THE EMPLOYMENT EQUALITY (AGE) REGULATIONS 2006

These regulations prohibited employers unreasonably discriminating against employees on grounds of age.

THE EQUALITY ACT (SEXUAL ORIENTATION) REGULATIONS 2007

These regulations prohibited discrimination on the grounds of sexual orientation, whether heterosexual, lesbian, gay or bisexual. Some exceptions included certain religious organizations which may restrict some of their activities or private clubs to selective membership, if this was in line with the main purpose of the club.

THE EQUALITY AND HUMAN RIGHTS COMMISSION 2007

The Equal Opportunities Commission, the Commission for Racial Equality and the Disability Rights Commission was disbanded in 2007 replaced by the Equality and Human Rights Commission.[31]

THE UN CONVENTION ON THE RIGHTS OF PERSONS WITH DISABILITIES 2008

The UN Convention on the Rights of Persons with Disabilities obliged all members to promote equal rights and root out discrimination, ratified by the UK government in 2010.

THE EQUALITY ACT 2010

The Equality Act 2010 consolidated all the previous 116 individual Acts and classified the nine characteristics protected by legislation.[32]

Claimants were able to make a discrimination claim on the basis of sex, race, disability, religion or philosophical belief, age, sexual orientation, gender reassignment, marriage and civil partnership plus pregnancy and maternity, without needing a qualifying period of employment.

Public Sector Equality Duty

The Equality Act 2010 introduced a duty on public sector organizations to consider all individuals when carrying out their day-to-day work, in shaping policy, delivering services and in relation to their employees. The duty requires public bodies to have due regard to the need to:

- Eliminate discrimination.
- Advance equality of opportunity.
- Foster good relations between different people.

Many public sector organizations will publish a report detailing their compliance with the Equalities Duty in meeting the three aims listed above after having completed an Equality Impact Assessment.

Positive action

Positive action is a legal option to address under-representation but is different to positive discrimination, which is considered unlawful.

Underrepresentation could be a council serving a diverse community, but not reflecting that diversity internally, or perhaps there is diversity in the council, but not among senior roles.

The three positive action options available to address under representation are:

1 Marginalized group(s) can be encouraged to apply for opportunities.

2 Providing targeted training/training places for marginalized groups(s).

3 In the event of a 'tiebreaker' during recruitment, where two applicants are equally suited and have scored the same, the person with the protected characteristic can be appointed.

2011 to 2019

THE MARRIAGE (SAME SEX) ACT 2013

Gay marriage becomes legal in England, Wales and Scotland but remained illegal in Northern Ireland until 2020. There was opposition to gay marriage from the Jewish, Muslim and Christian community due to being at odds with faith teachings and scriptures.

BREXIT 2016

Brexit, Britain's exit from the European Union was a divisive political act which set in motion far-right rhetoric focused on securing UK borders and tackling illegal immigration.

THE #METOO MOVEMENT 2017

The MeToo Movement started in 2006 and gained momentum in 2017 with the launch of the hashtag #MeToo.[33] Women felt empowered to speak up and come forward reporting cases of sexual abuse and harassment. The #MeToo, used by high-profile celebrities raised awareness with the underlying message being:

'Enough, No More!' #MeToo is seen as a rallying call for women, and consequently, more workplaces focus on tackling sexual harassment and abuse while also pushing for greater gender equity and respect.

THE GENDER PAY GAP 2017

Equality Act changes meant organizations with more than 250 employees are legally required to report their gender pay gap figures by the end of the financial year, including bonuses. The Chartered Institute of Personnel and Development (CIPD) explains that it compares men's and women's average (median) hourly rates of pay and 'provides a framework within which gender pay gaps can be surfaced'.[34]

Dean Royles clarifies, 'the gender pay gap is not the same as equal pay, it's the difference between the average pay of all men compared to the average pay of all women in an organisation'.[35]

The gender pay gap can be accompanied by a voluntary disclosure detailing how the organization intends to address it. This can be limited to a statement of intent without practical actions or accountability. Gender pay disparity was pushed up the agenda of senior leadership teams as a priority for the organization, motivated by pressure from stakeholders and the press calling it out. As it is an annual disclosure, year-on-year comparisons can be made to understand if it is improving or getting worse. It also means that organizations can be compared with others in the same industry and sector.

CLASSISM AS A PROTECTED CHARACTERISTIC 2019

A report commissioned by the British Psychological Society (BPS), highlighted how a person can be denied an opportunity based on their accent, postcode or any other indicator of their socio-economic background (refer to Chapter 3, 'Accent bias').[36] Research found that 50 per cent of jobseekers from lower socio-economic backgrounds feel recruitment processes are unfair towards them.[37] The Social Mobility Foundation noted that professionals from working-class backgrounds are paid over £6,000 less than higher-class employees in the same, exact roles.[38]

Several larger organizations like KPMG and EY recognize 'classism' as an issue and have taken active steps to attract and promote people from working-class backgrounds.[39] Those experiencing class discrimination only have the option of claiming unfair dismissal or a constructive dismissal claim, which requires a qualifying period of employment. The Trades Union Congress (TUC) proposed 'Classism' or 'Socio-Economic Class' to be categorized as a protected characteristic but failed.

2020 to 2025

GEORGE FLOYD'S MURDER 2020 AND BLACK LIVES MATTER (BLM)

The BLM movement[40] was founded in 2013, in response to police brutality and racially motivated violence against Black people in America, which resulted in the murder of Trayvon Martin, Michael Brown, Eric Garner, Rekia Boyd and others.

The murder of George Floyd in America in 2020, who was killed at the hands of a white police officer, turned BLM into a global stand against racism with many being able to relate to George Floyd's dying words, 'I can't breathe', in all aspects of their lives, including in the workplace. The global media attention led to many organizations focusing on racial equity and tackling barriers in the workplace, making anti-racism a priority.

SARAH EVERARD'S MURDER AND SUBSEQUENT PROTESTS 2021

Sarah Everard was raped, murdered and her body callously disposed of by Wayne Couzens, who had identified himself as an off-duty Metropolitan Police constable. It was a horrific crime, carried out by someone who was entrusted with law and order.

The Metropolitan Police came under criticism for failing to act against Couzens's previous allegations of indecent exposure, as well as its handling of the murder investigation. A review commissioned by the Metropolitan Police concluded that

Britain's largest police force is 'institutionally racist, misogynist and homophobic', and since the Macpherson Report, has 'remained largely white and largely male'.[41]

FORSTATER V CENTRE FOR GLOBAL DEVELOPMENT EUROPE 2022

The tribunal established being gender critical as a philosophical belief under the Equality Act 2010 but clarified this did not mean the belief could be expressed in a way that was discriminatory.[42]

DEFINITION OF SEX 2022

Under the Equality Act 2010, sex is understood as binary, with a person being male or female, and a person's legal sex being determined by what is recorded on their birth certificate, based on biological sex.

A trans person can legally change their sex by obtaining a Gender Recognition Certificate through procedures set out in the Gender Recognition Act 2004. A trans person who does not have a Gender Recognition Certificate retains the sex recorded on their birth certificate for legal purposes.

The Equality and Human Rights Commission (EHRC) published guidance[43] for service providers wishing to keep spaces as single-sex spaces, limiting them to biological males or biological females. This would include bathrooms or domestic abuse refuges, wherein it would not be illegal to bar transwomen or biological men from the refuge if females attending the refuge reported they were uncomfortable.

MENOPAUSE AS A PROTECTED CHARACTERISTIC 2023

Menopause affects all women at some point in their lives, usually between the ages of mid-40s to 50s. Symptoms range from low to severe intensity and impact each person differently. How organizations address menopause impacts how successful they are in attracting and retaining women, especially in an ageing work population.

The Women and Equalities Committee's 2022 report, 'Menopause and the workplace' found that women over the age of 50 represented the fastest-growing group in the workforce, and these highly skilled and experienced women were being pushed out of work due to employers' lack of support for menopausal symptoms.[44] Consequently, the Women and Equalities Committee proposed making menopause a protected characteristic, but the government argued existing protected characteristics of sex, age and disability already provide this protection.[45] They also thought it would discriminate against men with health conditions who would be treated differently.

THE WORKER PROTECTION ACT 2023

The Worker Protection Act 2023 has a duty for employers to prove they have taken all reasonable steps to prevent sexual harassment by employees, 'agents' and third parties in the workplace.

The EHRC Guidance 2024 clarified that employers will need to take a 'proactive' or 'anticipatory' approach to preventing sexual harassment in the workplace.[46] This differs from employer to employer, dependent on the size of the organization, resources available, and whether complaints have been raised previously. EHRC guidance advised assessing the risk of sexual harassment and having plans to reduce that risk. Failing to prevent sexual harassment can increase the amount of compensation paid to employees at tribunal by up to an extra 25 per cent.

THE NEONATAL CARE (LEAVE AND PAY) ACT 2023

Neonatal care leave allows parents, including fathers and partners, to have time off to be with a baby receiving neonatal care from the first day of work once their child has been in neonatal care for at least seven consecutive days.[47]

SUPREME COURT RULING ON GENDER 2025

The UK Supreme Court has clarified under the Equality Act 2010, the legal definition of a woman and sex refers to a biological woman and biological sex and confirmed the law still protects against discrimination against transgender people. This decision means that a biological man who identifies as a woman cannot use women-only spaces such as changing rooms, toilets, women's refuges, single-sex hospital wards and anywhere designated as for one sex only.

WHAT WOULD YOU DO?
Number 1

A recruiting manager approaches you after reviewing applicants for a new role and says, 'I don't see colour, gender or anything like that. I just pick the best person for the job. Everyone should be treated the same – that's equality, right?'

They let you know that they excluded one applicant because they did not see that person fitting in with the team.

- What are the concerns with this approach?

- What would you advise the recruiting manager?

CHAPTER SUMMARY

- Equality, Diversity and Inclusion are core concepts that need to be understood to be an effective EDI practitioner.

- The war for talent could be addressed by gaps in the demographic make-up in the workplace.

- The modern world of work was not constructed for marginalized groups.

- Equality legislation has evolved since the 1900s, and the Equality Act 2010 is one of the most crucial pieces of legislation to be aware of as an early career EDI practitioner.

- Global and political events have shaped societal views, creating a greater focus on certain protected characteristics.

REVIEW QUESTIONS

1 What is the difference between equality and equity?

2 Why are diverse teams good for productivity?

3 Can you list the nine protected characteristics?

4 What is the difference between equal pay and the gender pay gap?

Endnotes

1 https://www.collinsdictionary.com/dictionary/english/equality (archived at https://perma.cc/P9EG-JP9A)

2 https://www.merriam-webster.com/dictionary/diversity (archived at https://perma.cc/VK8U-MMDF)

3 https://dictionary.cambridge.org/us/dictionary/english/inclusion (archived at https://perma.cc/6FN5-GUCV)

4 Liddle, D (2021) *Transformational Culture*, Kogan Page, 209

5 Brann, A (2018) The Employee Experience, talk delivered at the Strategic HR Taskforce

6 https://www.hrmagazine.co.uk/content/news/nurse-who-was-left-out-of-a-tea-round-wins-payout-at-tribunal (archived at https://perma.cc/PMP6-Q6YX)

7 Maslow, A H (1943) A Theory of Human Motivation, *Psychological Review*, 50, 370–96

8 https://www.ons.gov.uk/peoplepopulationandcommunity/populationandmigration/populationestimates/datasets/populationestimatesforukenglandandwalesscotlandandnorthernireland (archived at https://perma.cc/C8PA-L2QM)

9 https://commonslibrary.parliament.uk/research-briefings/sn06838 (archived at https://perma.cc/AJ8L-DJUT)

10 https://www.gov.uk/government/collections/gender-equality-at-work-research-on-the-barriers-to-womens-progression (archived at https://perma.cc/9QFF-UX8N)

11 https://www.ons.gov.uk/peoplepopulationandcommunity/healthandsocialcare/healthandwellbeing/bulletins/disabilityenglandandwales/census2021 (archived at https://perma.cc/T6VE-NSRQ)

12 https://www.ons.gov.uk/peoplepopulationandcommunity/healthandsocialcare/disability/bulletins/disabilityandemploymentuk/2019 (archived at https://perma.cc/G8HC-4CL9)

13 https://www.ethnicity-facts-figures.service.gov.uk/uk-population-by-ethnicity/demographics/working-age-population/latest/#download-the-data (archived at https://perma.cc/X777-XPTL)

14 https://www.statista.com/statistics/1123370/unemployment-rate-in-the-united-kingdom-uk (archived at https://perma.cc/8MEZ-BVEH)

15 Michaels, E, Handfield-Jones, H and Axelrod, B (2001) *The War for Talent*, Harvard Business School Press

16 https://www.mckinsey.com/featured-insights/diversity-and-inclusion/diversity-matters-even-more-the-case-for-holistic-impact (archived at https://perma.cc/GB79-XDCA)

17 https://www.greatplacetowork.co.uk/best-workplaces/2024 (archived at https://perma.cc/S7R4-4RGG)

18 https://www.glassdoor.co.uk/Award/Best-Places-to-Work-UK-LST_KQ0,22.htm (archived at https://perma.cc/ZGT5-BBGG)

19 Taylor, F W (1911) *The Principles of Scientific Management*, Harper & Brothers

20 Fayol, H (1916) *Administration Industrielle et Générale*, Dunod

21 https://www.bbc.co.uk/news/uk-politics-51134644 (archived at https://perma.cc/2LUP-PHST)

22 https://www.bbc.co.uk/news/magazine-23795655 (archived at https://perma.cc/33FN-AA9Q)

23 https://www.birminghammail.co.uk/news/midlands-news/enoch-powell-what-rivers-blood-8945556 (archived at https://perma.cc/ET9S-GTTX)

24 https://www.history.com/topics/lgbtq/the-stonewall-riots (archived at https://perma.cc/8E2N-N6Y3)

25 https://www.legislation.gov.uk/ukpga/1970/41/enacted (archived at https://perma.cc/L3P7-HGHZ)

26   http://news.bbc.co.uk/1/hi/programmes/bbc_parliament/3631579.stm
     (archived at https://perma.cc/6GNP-8H3D)

27   https://www.stonewall.org.uk/about-us/our-history (archived at
     https://perma.cc/N9E7-U6VS)

28   https://www.independent.co.uk/news/uk/home-news/stephen-
     lawrence-murder-matthew-white-timeline-b2364160.html (archived
     at https://perma.cc/S89H-K5JA)

29   https://www.bbc.co.uk/news/explainers-54823810 (archived at
     https://perma.cc/XC3W-DAKF)

30   https://www.gov.uk/government/publications/the-stephen-lawrence-
     inquiry (archived at https://perma.cc/LC9B-RMGG)

31   https://www.equalityhumanrights.com/about-us (archived at
     https://perma.cc/S9E6-5U8A)

32   https://www.gov.uk/guidance/equality-act-2010-guidance (archived at
     https://perma.cc/G4SC-4GQM)

33   https://metoomvmt.org/get-to-know-us/history-inception (archived at
     https://perma.cc/Y66B-RCGG)

34   https://www.cipd.org/uk/knowledge/guides/what-is-the-gender-pay-
     gap (archived at https://perma.cc/8CUR-CMJW)

35   https://www.hrmagazine.co.uk/content/features/understanding-the-
     difference-between-equal-pay-and-gender-pay-gaps (archived at
     https://perma.cc/47PD-9ZV7)

36   https://www.lse.ac.uk/research/research-for-the-world/society/
     should-class-be-protected-under-law (archived at https://perma.cc/
     QYC9-JEHK)

37   https://www.hrmagazine.co.uk/content/news/half-from-
     disadvantaged-backgrounds-find-recruitment-unfair (archived at
     https://perma.cc/5CSF-7ZPT)

38   https://www.socialmobility.org.uk/news/class-pay-gap-day-2024
     (archived at https://perma.cc/W4DD-UL8S)

39   https://www.hrmagazine.co.uk/content/news/half-from-
     disadvantaged-backgrounds-find-recruitment-unfair (archived at
     https://perma.cc/5CSF-7ZPT)

40   https://blacklivesmatter.com/our-history (archived at
     https://perma.cc/5LCF-KGF2)

41 https://www.itv.com/news/london/2023-03-21/casey-report-what-are-the-key-findings-of-the-met-police-review (archived at https://perma.cc/U4VL-7R6P)

42 https://www.personneltoday.com/hr/maya-forstater-v-cgd-2022-judgment-transgender-gender-critrcal (archived at https://perma.cc/3ZK3-FLEC)

43 https://www.equalityhumanrights.com/media-centre/news/guidance-published-providers-single-sex-services (archived at https://perma.cc/J5VW-UYRL)

44 https://publications.parliament.uk/pa/cm5803/cmselect/cmwomeq/91/report.html (archived at https://perma.cc/E3JD-UN4A)

45 https://www.peoplemanagement.co.uk/article/1815996/government-right-reject-classifying-menopause-protected-characteristic (archived at https://perma.cc/KNT2-XVLJ)

46 https://www.hrmagazine.co.uk/content/news/new-ehrc-guidance-for-employers-on-preventing-sexual-harassment (archived at https://perma.cc/UQ2K-ZH66)

47 https://www.acas.org.uk/neonatal-care-leave-and-pay (archived at https://perma.cc/FD3J-7HYD)

CHAPTER TWO

HR's role in EDI

Introduction

In this chapter, we consider the relationship between HR and EDI, looking at traditional and more contemporary models of HR and how EDI fits into both. We look at HR's role in ensuring that people feel engaged, motivated and included in their organizations, how this aligns with EDI and should, ideally, align with the values and mission of an organization. Notions of belonging and being people-centric often underpin organizations' value statements.

EDI is a fast-growing discipline with numerous interconnected topics and jargon which must be understood to be an effective EDI practitioner. This chapter serves as a dictionary of key terms for you as an early career HR practitioner with an EDI remit. By absorbing them, you will appear knowledgeable and be able to unpick what people mean when they talk about concepts like a 'diversity hire' or 'psychological safety'.

We end the chapter by looking at your journey as an EDI practitioner within HR and ask whether you should consider a qualification to become a specialist. Certain skills and competencies are vital if you are to excel in the role. We look at what these are, so that you can consider your strengths as you progress throughout this book and any gaps you may need to fill.

LEARNING OBJECTIVES

By the end of this chapter, you will be able to:

• Understand how EDI relates to HR.

• Explain the meaning behind EDI terminology and jargon.

• Explore the options to get qualified as an EDI practitioner.

• Describe the skills needed to be an effective EDI practitioner.

The role of EDI within HR

This book has been written for the early career HR practitioner who has been tasked with looking after EDI in some capacity. It assumes that you are responsible in whole or part for EDI within your organization. HR plays a fundamental role in embedding EDI principles within the organization. As we will see throughout this book, the principles of EDI go across the employment lifecycle, from recruitment and selection to termination and everything in between.

HR, as a profession, is tasked with managing the employee lifecycle, compliance, payroll, personnel records and using HR Information Systems (HRIS). HR is often responsible for strategy and culture, managing change, leadership development, governance and producing data analytics. EDI usually falls within employee engagement, wellbeing and culture.

According to Frank Douglas, founder of Caerus Executive, the role of Chief Diversity Officer, at its highest level, is placed within HR, reporting to the Chief People Officer (CPO) or to the Head of Talent, who then reports to the CPO.[1] This, he argues, is too far down in the organizational hierarchy to be impactful. This, combined with the fact that EDI is often just one more thing on an already very long list of demands vying for HR's time, resources and attention, can contribute to a lack of progress and limited impact of EDI.

> **STOP AND THINK**
>
> Do some research in your own organization. Who is ultimately responsible for EDI, and who do they report to? Are they solely responsible for EDI, or do they have other responsibilities too?

The EDI value of values

The business case arguments for EDI speak volumes on their own merit, but they also most likely align with organizational values. Most organizations have carefully crafted 'vision and mission statements' – strategies that are underpinned by the organizational values which the senior leaders have collectively agreed are important to them.

These values often have buzzwords, such as: innovation, people-centric, empowerment, fairness, courage and authenticity. Some organizations have these words on the wall or in policy statements, and others articulate the behaviours expected concerning these values. Values can be a great way to underscore the relevance of EDI.

VALUED PEOPLE

Regardless of the values of an organization – stated or not – most will claim that their people are their most important resource or highest valued asset. Whether or not that is said as lip service, organizations can only deliver products and services through their people. Organizations are nothing more than a group of people following policies, processes and practices. So having an engaged, motivated workforce is a prerequisite to cost-effective and sustainable, long-term success, which brings the focus back to the importance of HR in ensuring that staff are feeling included and have a sense of belonging.

STOP AND THINK

EDI should not be an add-on or an 'instead of'. It should be aligned with the values of the organization. Think about your own organization's value statement. Does it include words that align with EDI?

Traditional and contemporary models of HR

It's useful for you to understand how different models of HR incorporate EDI. We'll start with Dave Ulrich's HR model, which is sometimes called the 'HR Business Partner' model.[2] Dave Ulrich is a thought leader in HR and proposed his model in the late 1990s. It became a foundational framework which has influenced the organization of HR functions across the private, public and voluntary sector. The model suggests HR has a strategic function through four distinct roles:

1 Strategic partner.
2 Change agent.
3 Administrative expert.
4 Employee champion.

Even though the model makes no direct reference to EDI, it clearly outlines areas where EDI can play a key role. As a 'strategic partner', HR can align EDI initiatives with business goals and the organizational strategy, with leadership being held accountable. As an 'employee champion', HR is positioned to be an advocate for minority groups within the workforce, creating inclusive cultures and psychological safety.

More contemporary models of HR, such as Perry Timms', 'HR 3.0' and David Liddle's 'People and Culture' model, position EDI more centrally. In his book *Transformational Culture*, Liddle states that 'Disparate disciplines of employee engagement, EDI and employee wellbeing compete against each other for resources, energy, time and focus. Yet, in virtually every possible respect, they complement each other. By bringing them together as a single, unified discipline, they act synergistically, with each area enhancing the other.'[3]

Timms shares his thoughts on how EDI fits within contemporary HR in the expert opinion box.

EXPERT OPINION

Perry Timms, Founder, People and Transformational HR Ltd and author of *The HR Operating Model, Transformational HR* and *The Energized Workplace*

EDI is both a philosophy and a science, integrated across all four areas of the HR 3.0 model – products, processes, systems and science. It embodies intersectionality within a progressive HR operating model, enabling all 'disciplines' in HR to foster stronger inclusion, deeper belonging and equitable experiences of work for all.

Creating inclusive cultures is a shared responsibility closely tied to organizational culture. The HR 3.0 model allows for a more multi-disciplinary approach to EDI to clarify, drive, intervene, assess and embed the philosophy of EDI into tangible actions, not housed in a role or function. So, we'd see Systems Designers using EDI as an embedded principle, People Operations creating accessible processes, avoiding any retrofit adjustments, impactful inclusion evidence provided by People Analysts and sustainable behavioural change driven by People Science Practice Leads.

With EDI (and wider culture, trust, wellbeing) ubiquitous in HR 3.0, it aims to usher in lasting, participative and fairer systems of work.

When tasked with EDI as an HR practitioner, you may find that people throw around terms that you, and perhaps not even they, fully understand. As an early career professional, it can be difficult to ask people to clarify what they mean, for fear of coming across as ignorant. In reality, you will find that people use terms without fully knowing their meaning, or terms can mean different things to different people. So never be afraid to ask someone to clarify the meaning behind their words.

The section that follows is an A to Z of key terms and topics you are likely to encounter. It's intended to be used as a quick reference guide, to help you when you come across something you don't fully understand. If a term is explained in detail somewhere else throughout this book, you will find a chapter cross-reference.

EDI topics and terminology

Like many technical specialisms, the world of EDI is awash with jargon that can be used to mystify and overinflate the discipline of EDI. Don't let this put you off. Use the below as a quick reference guide to decode what people are talking about.

Accessibility

Refer to Chapter 1. The Equality Act 2010 set out the duty to make reasonable adjustments to ensure that disabled people have equal access to information, goods and services.

Allyship

Refer to Chapter 5.

Authenticity versus conforming (or code switching)

'Be yourself, everyone is already taken', attributed to Oscar Wilde, is all that needs to be said on this topic. You should always be yourself unless your true self conflicts with the values and code of conduct in your organization (in which case, we need to have a different conversation). We only have experience of being ourselves (authenticity), and yet we suppress parts of our identity to be accepted (which is conforming).

Mercer's Global Talent Trends 2024[4] found that employees who felt comfortable bringing their authentic self to work are twice as likely to trust their organization and over five times more likely to be satisfied, with no intent to leave.

Authenticity is often listed as a key attribute of effective leaders. People feel more able to trust and follow a person who they see as being real, vulnerable and fallible, i.e. human! Employers recruiting for difference, should not expect a person to strip that difference away from themselves.

Acts of conforming (or masking) can be subtle. If our difference is linked to race, it could, for example, take the form of straightening hair. If our difference is linked to social class or regions, it could involve not speaking with an accent.

> **Code switching:** The 'switching back and forth' from our true authentic selves and the false identity we have created to fit into the workplace.

> **KEY POINT**
>
> It's difficult to be our true, authentic selves all of the time. We all participate in acts of conforming. It goes against the heart of EDI.

BIPOC

This is an acronym to signify Black, Indigenous and People of Colour and reflect racial identities other than white. It is sometimes referred to only as 'POC' – People of Colour.

Black Lives Matter movement

Refer to Chapter 1.

Cancel culture

Cancel culture occurs when a person says something or behaves in a way considered inappropriate and unacceptable within wider society. That person is effectively shunned, isolated and in some cases dismissed.

Being cancelled means you no longer have merit or currency in your professional discipline, or on public platforms such as social media.

It can be an overreaction to something unproven or without context, often reserved for celebrities and high-profile personalities. It can happen when someone says something out of ignorance or has simply been clumsy with language.

Fear of being cancelled can close genuine dialogue and prevent learning about difference.

Civil partnership

Refer to Chapter 1.

Cognitive diversity

Cognitive diversity refers to difference in thinking, which allows for differing perspectives and contributions to the workplace, suggesting there is no need for actual diversity.

The reality is that if everyone is from the same background, same gender, similar ages etc., they are likely to have had similar experiences in life and a tendency to have 'group think', thus stifling creativity and free thinking. For example, if members of a political party all have the same level of education and wages, they are more likely to agree on political stances.

Colour blindness

The phrase, 'I don't see colour' is usually well-intentioned and used to stress that any person is seen and valued, irrespective of their racial identity. Nevertheless, it would be inaccurate to state that the person's colour is not visible, when their colour is part of their identity and their lived experience.

Cultural appropriation

Typically, this occurs when an individual from a dominant culture adopts an element(s) of a minority culture, which causes offence to those from the minority culture. It is especially offensive when seen as inappropriate or when someone does not acknowledge the culture it originated from. An example is a white person taking elements from Black culture, such as wearing dreadlocks or speaking patwa, an English-based creole language spoken primarily in Jamaica.

> **KEY POINT**
>
> How do you distinguish between culture being appropriated and being appreciated and celebrated? It's a thin line between one and the other that depends on the context and how it is perceived.

Diversity hire

A diversity hire occurs when a person from a certain demographic is hired because the organization wants to increase representation to meet diversity targets, rather than because of their talents, experience and potential, and can be seen as a knee-jerk reaction to meet quotas. In practice, it can be counterproductive if little else is done to support and encourage a culture of inclusion and belonging, instead leading to tokenism. See also tokenism.

Employee resource groups (ERGs) or network groups

Refer to Chapter 5.

Equal pay claims

Refer to Chapter 1.

Equity audits and equality impact assessment

An equity audit is a systematic evaluation of structures, policies, practices and resources to ensure fairness and identify systemic barriers to equity and inclusion, focusing on long-term solutions rather than quick fixes. An equality impact assessment (EIA) is a structured process that is more singular in focus, examining how a policy, project, or decision might impact different marginalized groups and mitigate any negative impacts, which may not have been considered.

Gaslighting

Refer to Chapter 7.

Gender pay gap

Refer to Chapter 1.

Imposter syndrome

Imposter syndrome is a self-deprecating inner monologue, telling us that we are not good enough. This can especially be true for minorities who are aware of their difference, inducing a negative self-perception. This is fuelled by the superiority complex of others, resulting in a personal inferiority complex and self-limiting beliefs.

Intersectionality

When considering difference, it is usually limited to a single protected characteristic, for example, a targeted recruitment campaign to specifically attract women into the workplace.

However, we all differ across all of the protected characteristics, and people experience inequality uniquely based on these intersecting identities.

Aside from the stated protected characteristics, we have other differences, whether these are physical, such as our height and body shape, or our lived experiences. This could mean being from a certain class of people or having specific interests that are important and personal to us.

Intersectionality helps us to better understand how our vast differences as human beings create challenges and opportunities, barriers or privilege, therefore taking a holistic approach to EDI intervention. (For more on protected characteristics, refer to Chapter 1).

Lived experience

Our differing family relationships and social networks constantly influence the way we think and how we receive and process information to form our viewpoint.

We all have different talents and capabilities, which allow us to take advantage of opportunities or be denied them, due to internal and external barriers. Internal barriers are self-imposed, while external barriers could refer to a lack of resources, time and/or money.

We will hold certain things to be true, based on our lived experience, which shapes our thinking. There is great value in the lived experiences of marginalized individuals and groups as they can contribute essential insights into the organizational culture.

KEY POINT

Everyone's lived experience will be unique, so treat everyone as an individual.

LGBTQ+

LGBTQ+ is shorthand for lesbian, gay, bisexual, transgender and queer. Other acronyms exist such as LGBTQQIAAP, which additionally includes questioning, intersex, asexual, ally and pansexual.

#MeToo movement

Refer to Chapter 1.

Microaggressions

Refer to Chapter 7.

Neurodivergence

Neurodivergence is when someone's brain processes, learns and/or behaves differently and includes several conditions like autism, ADHD, dyslexia and dyspraxia.

Positive action or positive discrimination

Refer to Chapters 1 and 5.

Psychological safety

Psychological safety enables employees to be vulnerable, express themselves and their ideas, ask questions, challenge issues and raise concerns without fear of ridicule, reprisal, punishment or isolation.

This enables greater collaboration, participation and creativity, with individuals owning their mistakes, limiting a blame culture and encouraging a learning one.

Having psychological safety enables a person to be themselves and focus on the work, rather than worrying about others' opinions or unfair consequences.

A lack of psychological safety can enable an abuse of power, making safe spaces invaluable in building accountability.

Reasonable adjustments

Refer to Chapter 1.

Representation

Some organizations appoint diverse persons onto boards and senior leadership teams, which is good for representation and demonstrates that 'glass ceilings' can be broken, paving the way for others to follow.

However, being inclusive and championing belonging is not achieved simply through making appointments. Real representation, unlike tokenism, requires decision-making authority and visibility. It means being heard and having the freedom to be authentic without the need to conceal or conform.

> **Glass ceiling:** A phrase that describes an unofficial, usually unspoken barrier, preventing marginalized individuals progressing in their careers in an organization.

Restorative justice

Refer to Chapter 7.

Safe spaces

Safe spaces allow minorities to feel valued, supported and respected. The lack of hostility allows for freedom of expression without judgement, therefore encouraging dialogue, an exchange of ideas and learning, and the space to surface concerns. A safe space removes the need to conform and, where trust is built, enables people to feel empowered.

Safe spaces are an essential part of creating inclusive cultures in a workplace and can be physical environments, such as an office space, or virtual ones, like a WhatsApp group. Safe spaces can be used successfully by line managers, for example, choosing to arrange one-to-ones in a neutral place, such as a coffee shop, so long as the points of discussion are not confidential nor at risk of breaching GDPR.

A safe space is not exclusively linked to psychological safety, but psychological safety can be created by providing safe spaces.

Stereotypes

Refer to Chapter 3.

Stonewall riots and Stonewall organization

Refer to Chapter 1.

Systemic inequalities

Systemic inequalities are differences in treatment across healthcare, housing, education and employment, typically experienced by the working class and minorities.

Within the area of health, unequal access to quality healthcare can lead to higher rates of chronic illnesses and conditions, such as infant mortality. This can be because of bias in treatments, underrepresentation in clinical trials, or environmental factors, such as housing. For example, living in a home that is not heated or that is poorly ventilated can lead to respiratory conditions, resulting in sickness absence. This can impact a child's ability to attend school or a parent's ability to provide for the family.

Inequalities in education are caused by multiple factors. These can include schools that are poorly funded in low-income areas, which often serve minority students and may lead to lower academic achievements. Bias against the students and the lack of representation in teaching roles can exacerbate underachievement, affecting self-esteem, aspirations and opportunities in the workplace. Typically, good localities are where you will find good schools and vice versa.

Inequalities in the workplace exist at every stage of the employee lifecycle. We explore these in Chapters 6 and 7.

Systemic inequalities are also referred to as structural or institutionalized inequalities, but they have distinct nuances. In simple terms, 'systemic' refers to society-wide practices and 'structural' describes how systems interconnect, while 'institutionalized' is more focused within a single institution or organization.

> **KEY POINT**
>
> Inequalities are interconnected. One inequality has a detrimental effect on at least one other area. Addressing inequalities usually requires more than one intervention.

Tick-box exercise

A tick-box exercise is a disingenuous attempt to be seen to be doing the right thing, rather than committing time and resources to make a real difference. This can be more harmful and is often viewed with cynicism.

A tick-box approach is often seen on television shows and movies and involves casting an atypical lead actor with *insert difference* as a diverse supporting character.

Tokenism

Tokenism occurs when a minority is appointed to a senior role, but the appointment can be counterproductive. The selection and appointment of a minority person must be based on a meritocratic process. Otherwise, the lack of relevant qualifications, skills and experience could lead to poor performance.

If colleagues and peers believe that the individual was only appointed for being different, then this undermines the appointee.

There needs to be meaningful inclusion and empowerment, rather than an appointee being a 'poster child', brought out for corporate events.

Unconscious bias

Refer to Chapter 3.

Victim mentality (crying wolf)

A victim mentality means attributing everything perceived as potentially harmful or negative, to a protected characteristic. For example, believing that a promotion was denied because of gender, or a redundancy was made due to sexual orientation. This can be harmful when trying to create inclusive workplaces.

Minorities can be targeted unfairly for inequitable treatment, purely because of their protected characteristic(s), but not everything is related to a protected characteristic in every situation.

Consequently, employers may refrain from recruiting diverse employees out of fear of being labelled for tackling genuine performance issues. They may also fear saying something inappropriate, out of ignorance, thus resulting in a grievance or being cancelled.

KEY POINT

'Crying wolf' every time anything happens risks the employer not taking the person seriously when something happens that is related to the person's difference.

Virtue signalling

Virtue signalling is effectively declaring, 'Hey, look at us, aren't we great?' It means showcasing what is being done on an EDI issue or showing solidarity with a minority group with the intention of creating a positive marketing campaign, as part of the employer branding, to attract and retain talent.

Virtue signalling means being more concerned with perception, rather than doing anything meaningful and sustainable to support a cause or a group of people.

Virtue signalling can be misleading, such as featuring diverse actors on a corporate website despite there being a lack of diversity internally and a struggle to hire and retain diverse staff.

White fragility

White fragility, a term coined by Robin DiAngelo, who wrote a book about race relations in the US, refers to a defensive reaction such as denial, anger or discomfort that some white individuals may feel when discussing racism and white privilege.[5]

White fragility led to the hashtag #WhiteLivesMatter and #AllLivesMatter which is like stating that all trees matter, when it is the Amazon rainforest at risk due to deforestation.

White privilege

The term 'white privilege' was popularized during the Black Lives Matter movement.

The inference of the term is that a white person, by virtue of their skin colour, has an unearned privilege in society, thus enabling them to have better access to more opportunities. The term is unhelpful as it can end up negating the hard work and the sacrifices made to attain career opportunities and development.

A more appropriate term would be 'unearned advantages and societal benefits', which, unlike white privilege, is not limited to skin colour and could be any of the following, e.g. name, gender, social class, accent, family, height etc.

A non-white comparator is more likely to experience systemic inequalities, more barriers and have fewer opportunities, so will need to sacrifice more, work harder and longer just to keep up, let alone excel.

Henley Business School research[6] found that white privilege in the UK workforce is very real, showing that Black employees are worse off than those from a white background in the labour market. The Cabinet Office found that around 1 in 10 adults from a Black, Pakistani, Bangladeshi or mixed background were unemployed, compared to 1 in 25 white British people.[7]

Wilful blindness

Wilful blindness occurs when a person intentionally avoids acknowledging facts and information they could or should be aware of. By choosing not to see or address the problem, they create a form of self-imposed ignorance hoping perhaps the problem will go away or sort itself out.

Windrush generation

See Chapter 1.

Woke (agenda)

Wokeness, as a concept, became popular during the American civil rights movement. Being woke meant you had woken up to historical racial abuse, hence the hashtag, #StayWoke, but has since broadened to include various social issues, such as sexism, LGBTQ+ rights and the environment.

The 'woke agenda' is used by critics and detractors to describe initiatives or ideologies that are seen as politically left-wing and progressive. The detractors view the 'woke agenda' as a disingenuous attempt to be politically correct, carrying out performative activism and virtue signalling.

STOP AND THINK

Before we continue, pause for a moment and reflect on the terms and concepts you have just learned about:

- How many were familiar to you before you read this chapter?
- Has your understanding of any of them changed?
- Can you think of examples of any of these concepts from your own experience, either within or outside work?

Your journey as an EDI practitioner

The CIPD found that only 1 in 10 people practitioners come from ethnic backgrounds.[8] Additionally, while 60 per cent of the profession is female and 40 per cent is male, this is flipped when looking at leadership roles, where 61 per cent are male and 39 per cent female. So what does this tell us? HR, as a profession, is primarily white and female, except for senior roles, which are disproportionately held by white men. Ironically, HR is tasked to address EDI challenges while suffering from the same challenges themselves.

STOP AND THINK

Consider your own organization, and your position within it. Are the CIPD stats about gender and race reflected in your HR function? Is it predominantly female and white, with the top spots mainly reserved for white men?

TOP TIP
'Heal thyself'

Like the physician being told to 'heal thyself', HR too needs to fix itself, in addition to tackling the wider workplace. As you progress in your career and perhaps become responsible for building a team, bear this point in mind.

Becoming an EDI specialist

There are many EDI specialists, but none can be regarded as experts, as there is no benchmark or standards to meet. Many EDI leads 'fall' into this specialist space because they have shown an interest in advocating for a particular strand of diversity or have a certain protected characteristic themselves. These

EDI leads are often from ethnic backgrounds, and are female, and/or gay, and/or disabled, but are all still learning in a discipline that has grown considerably.

TOP TIP
Further your learning in EDI

Search out relevant programmes, courses and modules on EDI to help further your learning and become an EDI specialist.

Organizations such as the CIPD and Chartered Management Institute (CMI) provide a range of learning opportunities of varying lengths and durations.

Keeping abreast of EDI articles in publications such as *People Management Magazine*, *HR Magazine*, *Personnel Today*, *HR Zone* and *People Space* will help you keep up-to-date on EDI. Remember that the world of EDI is forever evolving.

Skills and competencies for EDI work

It's useful for you to develop certain skills and attributes as you progress along your EDI path. Much of what we discuss below is not only relevant to EDI work, but to being an effective HR practitioner generally. They will enable greater success in your ability to provide support and deliver on your mandate.

We will return to these skills and competencies again in the Conclusion, when you will have the opportunity to reflect on your current abilities and identify any gaps you need to fill.

MINDSET

The right mindset is critical and underpins everything else. The US psychologist Carol Dweck suggests that we either have a 'fixed' or 'growth' mindset.[9]

A fixed mindset assumes that things will always be the way they are, and nothing will ever change. This mindset becomes a self-fulfilling prophecy. A growth mindset assumes that irrespective of how things are right now, they can change for the better. 'I can't do this' (fixed mindset), becomes 'I can't do this yet' (growth mindset). The former is a self-limiting belief, while the latter frees the person to bring about change.

TOP TIP
Develop a growth mindset

Working in EDI requires a growth mindset because, irrespective of where an organization is in terms of its maturity and understanding, there will always be more that can be done. See problems as opportunities and create solutions.

EMPATHY

Empathy is a superpower which enables connection with others by seeing the world through their eyes. Leaders who demonstrate empathy promote trust and inclusion, but a lack of empathy can potentially add to misunderstandings, alienation and systemic inequities.

Empathy is crucial in mitigating prejudice and fostering social harmony through exposure to diverse perspectives. Some of us are naturally more empathetic than others, but like any other skill, it can be developed through practices like mindfulness and emotional intelligence training.

CURIOSITY

Being and staying curious is an essential skill for EDI practitioners, partially because there is so much to know in EDI, and partially because you will need to have a genuine interest in people to explore difference from a positive standpoint.

Asking the simple, obvious questions is always a great starting point: what, who, where, when, why and how. If you ask these questions about topics, about people and their lived experiences, and about the organization itself, you will better understand what the issues are and be in a better position to see possible solutions. Being curious will also help you to build your business case (Refer to Chapter 8).

CULTURAL INTELLIGENCE OR COMPETENCY (CQ)

CQ is a relatively new concept but no less important than intelligence quotient (IQ) and emotional intelligence (EQ).

> **Intelligence quotient:** Typically, intelligence was measured through academic achievement as an indicator of potential within the workplace.

> **Emotional intelligence:** Emotional intelligence has become increasingly important, especially in complex working environments, as it is the ability to regulate and manage your own emotions and the emotions of others.

CQ is the ability to understand, communicate with, and effectively interact with people across different cultures. It is particularly useful in global workplaces. Having a high level of CQ enables deeper human connection, preventing cultural appropriation and clumsy, inappropriate language.

SELF-AWARENESS

'Know thyself', attributed to Socrates, is a deeply profound statement. Being self-aware is important in every context, and particularly in the discipline of EDI.

You will have certain life experiences and networks that will have shaped your thinking, and this will inevitably impact your approach to addressing issues around EDI. There may be a certain strand of difference that you favour, because perhaps you share that difference or characteristic, or you can relate to it in some way, but equally, there may be a strand of difference that you are less comfortable with or less adept with.

Forewarned is forearmed. Being self-aware will help to keep you balanced and focused. That's not to say you will be unbiased and completely fair, but knowing you have a certain leaning will assist you while you grow your own understanding and empathy for others. For more on unconscious bias, refer to Chapter 3.

NUMERACY SKILLS

While number crunching was probably not the reason you entered the people profession, data can be your best friend. Aim to increase your numerical proficiency. The ability to analyse data to identify trends, track diversity metrics and assess the impact of EDI initiatives will turn you into an EDI 'rock star'. For more, refer to the section in Chapter 8, 'Metrics that matter'.

COMMUNICATION SKILLS

Being able to articulate the case for EDI to receive senior leadership support is essential. This means being able to communicate both orally and in written form, as well as being able to present ideas, outputs and outcomes. Refer to the section in Chapter 8 on 'Soft power'.

As a person working in EDI, you need to be able to advocate for marginalized groups and influence the senior leadership team's agenda. As your career progresses, you will likely need to encourage open discussions, challenge bias and discrimination and, depending on funding, you may even need to deliver training internally. Relax, you got this (growth mindset).

WHAT WOULD YOU DO?
Number 2

An employee has reportedly said your organization's EDI training is 'woke' and is vocally sharing this view with colleagues, disparaging the training and the organization.

- What are the concerns with the employee's views?
- What would you advise the employee?

CHAPTER SUMMARY

- EDI is an essential part of HR across the employee lifecycle, from recruitment to termination. It usually sits within employee wellbeing and culture.

- Get familiar with EDI terminology and jargon. It will help you to stand out in conversations about EDI. If people are using these terms incorrectly, or their meaning is unclear, don't be afraid to ask them to clarify what they are saying.

- Numerous options are available to become qualified as an EDI practitioner. Explore organizations such as CIPD and CMI to see what they can offer.

- Certain skills and competencies stand out as being vital to thriving in an HR career. Consider those discussed in this chapter and any that you might need to develop further.

REVIEW QUESTIONS

1 Where does EDI fit in traditional and contemporary models of HR?

2 Can you explain why only Black lives matter?

3 What EDI challenges does HR have as a function?

4 What skills do you need to be an effective EDI practitioner?

Endnotes

1 https://www.hrmagazine.co.uk/content/news/is-chief-diversity-officer-a-ceiling-for-black-employees (archived at https://perma.cc/6E4E-HL6R)

2 Ulrich, D (1997) *Human Resource Champions: The next agenda for adding value and delivering results*, Harvard Business School Press
3 Liddle, D (2021) *Transformational Culture*, Kogan Page, 199
4 https://www.mercer.com/assets/global/en/shared-assets/local/attachments/pdf-2024-global-talent-trends-report-en.pdf (archived at https://perma.cc/74RJ-5V2E)
5 DiAngelo, R (2019) *White Fragility: Why it's so hard for white people to talk about racism*, Penguin Books
6 https://www.henley.ac.uk/news/2021/new-research-explores-racial-equity-in-uk-businesses (archived at https://perma.cc/C6CY-99AD)
7 https://assets.publishing.service.gov.uk/media/5a9ec73a40f0b64d7d48f2b7/Revised_RDA_report_March_2018.pdf (archived at https://perma.cc/9JTZ-JPCB)
8 https://www.hrmagazine.co.uk/content/news/hr-profession-still-lacking-diversity/ (archived at https://perma.cc/B3HL-3F88)
9 Dweck, C S (2006) *Mindset: The new psychology of success*, Random House

CHAPTER THREE

Biases and behaviour

Introduction

We all have biased thinking, which is not necessarily right or wrong; it is just our thinking at a specific point in time. We all have things which we either love or hate, a favourite or least favourite football team, movie, family member, food item, dress sense, friend, work colleague, restaurant or song. This biased thinking is not necessarily hard-wired but can take a fair bit of work to revise.

This chapter will help you explore your biases and understand the critical importance of recognizing bias in the workplace. It covers conscious and unconscious bias, the harmful practice of stereotyping and how to overcome bias, by recognizing and altering how you think. Ultimately, this chapter will not only help you to understand yourself, it will also help you to spot and formulate appropriate responses to bias in the workplace.

LEARNING OBJECTIVES

By the end of this chapter, you will be able to:

- Understand what bias is and how it affects us all.
- Appreciate that stereotypes are mostly harmful.

- Self-assess biased associations.
- Identify several types of bias and how they impact decision-making and behaviours.
- Understand your brain from the point of view of Systems 1 and 2 thinking.

What is conscious and unconscious bias?

Bias refers to having a mindset or world view derived from one's own lived experiences and immediate influences. This bias impacts our attitudes, understanding, actions and decisions.

While this chapter is primarily about unconscious bias, it is important to note that not all bias is unconscious. A person may be consciously biased, so they are fully aware of what is driving their thinking and behaviour.

> **Unconscious bias (also known as implicit bias)**: A bias we are not always cognisant of, present to varying degrees and which surfaces in our behaviours and actions.

EDI efforts focus on fostering greater self-awareness through training to help recognize and mitigate the impact of unconscious bias in the workplace. It is unrealistic to expect to eliminate bias completely because it will still show up in our words and actions.

Let us explore biases by considering cats and dogs. Someone who had a bad experience with a dog as a child (or a perceived bad experience, such as a boisterous, playful dog rather than a vicious one) is likely to favour cats over dogs as an adult. However, someone else who had a cat lash out at them when they were a child may well favour dogs over cats as an adult. We are not born with an affinity towards cats or dogs, but it can develop through our lived experiences. And these perspectives can shift, depending on new experiences. Someone who is nervous around dogs will not necessarily feel that way forever – they may get to know a dog who puts them at their ease, and the way they feel may start to shift.

This is also true for our biases against one another. In *The Long Walk to Freedom*,[1] Nelson Mandela wrote that 'No one is born hating another person because of the colour of his skin, or his background, or his religion. People must learn to hate, and if they can learn to hate, they can be taught to love, for love comes more naturally to the human heart than its opposite.'

Stereotypes

To be stereotypical is to form a view of a whole community, based on your own experience with someone from that community, or based on typically held views, which are often promoted in pop culture and social circles.

The truth is no single individual, good or bad or indifferent, is representative of a whole population, even when there are shared characteristics. We are all uniquely different. No one person is like another. Even identical twins have differences. When we take the view 'so and so' must think, act and behave a certain way because they are A, B or C, then we are reducing the whole community to a caricature, doing a disservice to the individual and the wider group.

This type of reduction surfaces linguistically when you hear someone say, 'I never thought "X" would do "Y"... that's not like them', or 'I thought all "A's" do that... they must be the exception' or 'I don't like "XXX" I don't know why... I just don't... it's just a gut feeling'.

Stereotypes are reductive, lazy, inaccurate and often harmful. Stereotyping is lazy because we are not taking the time to see the person.

STOP AND THINK

Solve the following riddle.

A father is driving his son to the airport. The son has a scheduled flight to another city, and the father wants to see him safely off. They arrive together at the airport; the son checks his luggage in and has a bite to eat with his father, before then going through the security checks to catch his plane. The father stays at the airport, and only after seeing his son's plane leave does he decide to leave.

During the flight, the son starts to feel very unwell, so after the plane lands, he is rushed into hospital. The doctor sees him brought into the accident and emergency department, and exclaims loudly, 'Oh my God, that's my son'!

How is this possible?

Explanations include the following:

- The father was driving his stepson to the airport.

- The father was driving his adopted son to the airport.

- The son never got on the plane.

- The plane was diverted back to the point of departure, so was seen by the father at a local hospital.

- The doctor made a mistake.

- The son has an identical twin brother.

Our guesses reveal our bias. The doctor was the mother. It's obvious when you stop and think about it. Many of us are influenced by our bias without even realizing it.

Biased associations

Biased associations happen when a stereotyped behaviour is associated with a group of people who share a common characteristic, for example, gender or race. They are like mental shortcuts that we make that we associate with certain groups.

The boxed example demonstrates a biased association in relation to gender. When you have read it, complete the exercise to explore any biased associations you might have.

EXAMPLE

Are men or women better drivers (taking 'better' to mean having fewer fatal accidents on the road that involve more than one vehicle)? The answer depends on who is answering the question. Many people would think they could give you a definitive answer without thinking about it, but research shows that the answer isn't clear-cut:

- Men are twice as likely to have fatal accidents as women when driving cars, and four times as likely when trucks are involved.[2]

- Women are involved in more bus-related fatalities when driving buses, compared to men. Women are also less likely to make an insurance claim and less likely to commit offences related to driving, but this could be because it takes women longer to get their licenses, meaning they have more practice. And while more women take their driving test than men, fewer pass.[3]

So who are the better drivers, men or women?

EXERCISE

Explore your own biased associations. Based on your experience, complete the following sentence.

Women/men are usually... ?

Now replace 'women/men' with one or more of the groups from the following list and complete the sentence again.

- Blacks/Whites/Asians.
- Young/old people.

- Disabled people.

- Muslims/Christians/Jews.

- Immigrants.

- Heterosexuals/homosexuals.

- Anorexic/obese people.

- Terrorists.

- Tall/short people.

How many biased associations did you make?

TOP TIP
Google Project Implicit

Project Implicit is a research initiative from Harvard University, the University of Virginia and the University of Washington, which studies implicit biases people may hold, revealed through their associations and attitudes.

To arrive at a view, the Implicit Association Test (IAT) is conducted on an online platform that measures preferences or biases across several topics, including protected characteristics, like race, gender and age.

The test is free of charge and is useful for self-assessment by encouraging critical thinking around your own biases to help address prejudice and discrimination.

The IAT measures the strength of associations between groups of people and stereotypes by asking you to quickly sort words into categories on the left-hand or right-hand side, by pressing the 'e' key, or the 'i' key on the keyboard.

The IAT can reveal whether you have a harmful association with a particular type of person.

Each test only takes a few minutes, but may go some way in explaining some of those biased associations you may have made earlier.

Types of bias

Numerous biases occur in the workplace and our daily lives. The bad news is that these biases can work in conjunction with one another. There are many more[4] than the ones listed in this section, which means this can be a difficult area to navigate, but not impossible.

Beauty bias

'Beauty is in the eye of the beholder'. If we find someone aesthetically attractive, we treat them favourably, but if we find them unattractive, then we treat them unfavourably. This is also known as 'pretty privilege'.

Height and hair colour have nothing to do with competence and potential, but research demonstrates that height correlates with higher income.[5] Recruiters favour taller candidates, and height influences promotion opportunities. We perceive taller men and women as more 'leader-like', deeming them to be more dominant, intelligent and healthier; tall men are more likely to attain managerial positions.

'Blondes have more fun'. Whether true or not, findings suggest women with blonde hair are more likely to become CEOs, according to the University of British Colombia, while comparatively blonde males only account for 2 per cent of CEOs.[6] Studies have also found that women with blonde hair enjoy an earnings premium.[7]

Horned and halo effect

The 'Horned (devil) Effect' arises from negative assumptions and judgements about a person. No matter what person A does, they can do nothing right and are held accountable for the smallest issue.

The 'Halo (angel) Effect' perceives a person more positively than deserved. No matter what person B does, they can do no wrong and will receive only the mildest reprimand, if anything at all.

In the workplace, the Horned/Halo effect means two people can do the same piece of work to the same standard. One will have their mistakes and failings pointed out, with their work never being good enough, while the other is rewarded and celebrated. For example, two people can both arrive late to work, but only one is constantly reprimanded. These effects lead to unfair treatment and unjust outcomes.

Affinity bias

Affinity bias is about preferring people who are similar to ourselves, whether through gender, ethnicity, age range, social class, beliefs or interests. We feel less threatened surrounded by 'more of the same' individuals, with those we think we have common ground with and shared lived experiences, often ignoring or overlooking shortcomings.

In the same way that we form friendships with those we feel affinity with, we might also allow this bias to influence our hiring decisions in the workplace. Affinity bias occurs in many senior leadership teams, which end up 'White, male and stale'. Remember the quote attributed to General George S Patton, 'If everyone is thinking alike, then somebody isn't thinking'. The result means fewer new ideas, less critical analysis, limited innovation and reduced problem-solving skills. This limits growth and taking advantage of new opportunities.

Having similar outlooks can create echo chambers, reflecting views already held to be true and, more importantly, reinforcing each other as having the correct position. This results in a 'herd' mentality, often seen in large assemblies, such as the storming of the Capital Building, Washington DC in 2021, which was driven by the belief that the election had been 'stolen' and this messaging was then amplified.

> **KEY POINT**
>
> It is more comfortable and easier to deal with people who are all 'cut from the same cloth', as there is less conflict. This, however, comes with the risk of 'groupthink'.

Attribution and confirmation bias

Attribution bias involves attributing your own judgements to the actions of others. For example, Person X arrives late every day, and you conclude that this person must be lazy.

There may be several reasons for the lateness:

- Person X has agreed a late start every day with their manager, with hours made up later.
- Person X is on a reduced-hour work pattern.
- Person X has caring responsibilities and is regularly delayed due to unforeseen issues, but has discussed this with their line manager.
- Person X has a medical condition and has agreed a later start time as a reasonable adjustment with their line manager.

Confirmation bias involves 'doubling down' on a previously held belief.

In the example of Person X being late, it may be noted that they do not wear a wristwatch, which reinforces the fact that they do not respect time, thus confirming that they must be lazy. The reason Person X does not wear a watch could vary:

- Person X relies on their mobile phone to keep track of time, setting reminders to meet targets and deadlines.
- Person X has a medical condition, and wearing a watch can cause a flare-up.
- Person X has never worn a watch, so sees no reason to start now.

> **TOP TIP**
> Just ask
>
> Have a conversation to understand colleagues rather than pass judgements based on incomplete information.

Conformity bias

We considered conformity bias in Chapter 2 when exploring authenticity versus conforming (or code-switching). We will return to it again in Chapter 4, in relation to the Asch Conformity Experiment.

Conformity bias involves changing one's beliefs or behaviours in the hope of being accepted by others. One's own judgement and thinking are abandoned, even when it makes little sense or is detrimental.

Conformity bias takes the form of peer pressure to fit in, to go with the habits and practices of others, to give up your own thoughts and position in favour of the group, as this is seen as the norm, and there is a fear of being viewed as different. An example could be that Person A goes out with a group of friends, even though Person A does not want to go out, but wants to feel included and part of the friendship group.

In the workplace, you may have a question following a presentation from a senior leader, however, if the normal practice is not to ask any questions, then more than likely, you will stay quiet. You let your question go unanswered to avoid the risk of being the odd one out.

> **TOP TIP**
> Be yourself
>
> Conforming means losing a bit of yourself. We all 'cave in' on different issues at different points in our lives. It does take time

and maturity to be comfortable with who you are, but eventually, you realize you are already enough.

Proximity bias

We tend to favour individuals who are closer to us physically, regarding how we choose to spend our time. In the workplace, this can lead to preferential treatment for those we work closely with to the detriment of others. In hybrid working, this can be notable with those who are physically in the workplace being rewarded and recognized as opposed to those working remotely or flexibly. In this case, out of sight really is out of mind.

Accent bias

A typical villain, as depicted in Hollywood, often has an English, Russian or Middle Eastern accent. The implication is clear and is used to demarcate the 'good guys' from the 'bad guys', but this creates an association in our minds as part of our socialization and conditioning entirely based on racist tropes.

A 2022 Northumbria University study found that people with Northern accents were presumed to be less intelligent, ambitious and educated, but were also regarded as friendly, outgoing and trustworthy.[8] Research by the University of Cambridge and Nottingham Trent University 2025 suggested that people with regional accents, i.e. from Liverpool, Newcastle, Bradford and London, are more likely to have committed a crime and to be victims of injustice.[9]

Accents should not be taken as a measure of intelligence, academic success or behaviours, but nevertheless, accent bias is very real, leading some to hide their accent in order to be accepted and progress in their careers.

Artificial intelligence bias

It is difficult to avoid artificial intelligence (AI), and it can be invaluable in collating, analysing and understanding information. It is often increasingly being used by employers to assess job applications.

Although AI is intended to be objective, it can inadvertently reinforce or amplify societal biases. AI models are trained on large datasets reflecting the real world, which includes social inequalities or discriminatory patterns and therefore, can result in data bias. For example, facial recognition systems have had higher error rates identifying Black or Asian individuals, due to training data predominantly featuring lighter-skinned faces.

Developers may unintentionally build systems that disadvantage certain groups. For example, Amazon scrapped an AI recruiting tool because it discriminated against female applicants. This is because the algorithm had been trained on past hiring data in a male-dominated tech industry.

Search engines powered by AI can also demonstrate bias. A study by Latanya Sweeney, from Harvard University, found proof of discrimination in online ad delivery, with names commonly associated with Black individuals more likely to display criminal record ads, thus reinforcing harmful stereotypes.[10]

AI language models can perpetuate discriminatory language patterns. For example, language models have been shown to associate certain job titles with specific genders or produce harmful stereotypes in their outputs.

In summary, AI, just like human intelligence, can be discriminatory and biased.

Understanding our behaviour

In 2012, psychologist Daniel Kahneman published a book called *Thinking, Fast and Slow*.[11] The main takeaway of the book is that our brains have two ways of thinking and processing

information, known as 'systems'. System 1 and System 2 thinking are done in different parts of the brain:

- System 1 is very fast and unconscious. It is effortless, intuitive
  and automatic, without self-awareness or control.
- System 2 is comparatively slow and conscious. It is deliberate,
  takes effort, and is a controlled mental process, with self-
  awareness and logic.

Given the fast-paced nature of general life and work, with multiple priorities and pressures to perform and deliver meeting
deadlines, System 1 thinking is invaluable. System 1 thinking
allows us to respond in the moment, make decisions and act,
moving from one issue to the next without slowing down.
However, an overreliance on System 1 thinking risks us making
assumptions and missing things. If you initially assumed that
the parent doctor in the earlier example was male, you were
using System 1 thinking. Sometimes, we need to use our System
2 thinking to slow down and really consider things carefully.

Systems 1 and 2 thinking and first impressions

According to research,[12] when we meet someone for the first
time, we form a view about them, their competence and trust-
worthiness etc., within milliseconds. This is thought to be
engaging our survival instinct, which evaluates potential friends
or foes, using System 1 thinking.

The Guardian newspaper ran an advert titled, 'Points of
View', underscoring how quickly we form a view based on
seconds of information and arrive at an incorrect view of what
is happening.[13] The advert involves a young man, dressed in a
manner associated with 'skinheads', running down the street.
The scene from one angle depicts the 'skinhead' appearing to
grab the briefcase of a man dressed in a business suit. The
same scene from a wider perspective reveals that the man in

the business suit is in danger from falling construction materials overhead and the 'skinhead' is pushing him out of harm's way.

System 1 thinking leads us to categorize people by labels, as a means of shorthand, and is usually accompanied by stereotypes: disabled, divorced, poor, old, overweight, Hispanic, female, young, Black, stupid and the list goes on.

As stated earlier, we are all complex individuals, so no one single label will ever do us justice and yes, it takes more conscious effort to go beyond a label and learn more about the wonderful human being in front of you.

If your initial view is based on the first few milliseconds, how reliable can it be?

System 2 thinking requires us to literally slow down and think critically. It is much more tiring than System 1 thinking, but allows us to analyse, reflect and consider information in a more meaningful way, a luxury we do not afford ourselves often enough.

WHAT WOULD YOU DO?
Number 3

A manager shares with you that she regards Ayesha, a hijab-wearing young woman on the autistic spectrum, as quiet and not very assertive, lacking leadership potential.

- What concerns do you have about the manager's views?
- What would you advise the manager?

Think about the use of Systems 1 and 2 thinking in your answer.

CHAPTER SUMMARY

- Every single person has a different lived experience, so a person's bias can vary, and not all bias is unconscious.
- Stereotyping involves attributing a range of qualities, mostly negative, to that whole community of people.

- Self-assessing one's own biased associations exposes areas for learning and development.
- Several types of bias impact our decision-making and behaviours.
- System 1 thinking is fast and automatic, often relying on unconscious biases, while System 2 thinking involves deliberate and analytical processing, which can counteract these biases.

REVIEW QUESTIONS

1 What is a biased association?
2 Name three different types of bias that are relevant to workplaces.
3 Is System 1 thinking conscious or unconscious?

Endnotes

1 Mandela, N (1994) *Long Walk to Freedom*, Little Brown and Company
2 https://injuryprevention.bmj.com/content/injuryprev/27/1/71.full.pdf (archived at https://perma.cc/GZW7-WZDH)
3 https://news.sky.com/story/women-are-better-drivers-than-men-study-finds-11484839 (archived at https://perma.cc/A7SF-EE7Q)
4 https://asana.com/resources/unconscious-bias-examples (archived at https://perma.cc/C6AR-3LXY)
5 https://www.bbc.com/worklife/article/20220825-height-discrimination-how-heightism-affects-careers (archived at https://perma.cc/S8NZ-X6AS)
6 https://graziadaily.co.uk/life/real-life/blondes-higher-career-chances-ceo/ (archived at https://perma.cc/GBG2-RBPV)
7 Gueguen, N (2012) Hair Color and Wages: Waitresses with blond hair have more fun, *Journal of Socio-Economics*, 41(2), 370–72

8 https://www.northumbria.ac.uk/about-us/news-events/news/new-research-reveals-prejudice-against-people-with-northern-english-accents/ (archived at https://perma.cc/NKB2-8WC5)

9 https://www.northumbria.ac.uk/about-us/news-events/news/new-research-reveals-prejudice-against-people-with-northern-english-accents/ (archived at https://perma.cc/NKB2-8WC5)

10 https://papers.ssrn.com/sol3/papers.cfm?abstract_id=2208240 (archived at https://perma.cc/UT5H-Y5DF)

11 Kahneman, D (2012) *Thinking, Fast and Slow*, Penguin Random House

12 Willis, J and Todorov, A (2006) First Impressions: Making up your mind after a 100-ms exposure to a face, *Psychological Science*, 17(7), 592–98

13 https://youtu.be/_SsccRkLLzU (archived at https://perma.cc/54AU-NBH3)

CHAPTER FOUR

Social conditioning and fear

Introduction

In his book, *Transformational Culture*, David Liddle notes that, 'Exclusion feeds division, which in turn feeds intolerance, which in turn feeds hate.'[1] A fear of difference inevitably leads to suffering, whether we refer to the UK race riots in 2024 or innocent people around the world being oppressed and persecuted for being 'the other'.

To understand fear of difference, we must first grasp the often irrational nature of fear itself. We begin this chapter by considering some examples of rational and irrational fears, and the impact of being taught to fear strangers as children. Childhood stories have taught us to fear the unknown or the 'different', embedding this fear into our subconscious from an early age. This social conditioning makes it challenging to embrace diversity without hesitation or prejudice, thus hindering our ability to genuinely appreciate and celebrate the richness of human difference.

Social conditioning does not stop with our formative years. Adults can be influenced to think and behave in specific ways by influences in society and the media.

We end this chapter by looking at some psychological experiments that demonstrate how we can be conditioned to act against our better nature, in ways that may be discriminatory and harmful.

LEARNING OBJECTIVES

By the end of this chapter, you will be able to:

- Understand types of fear and the negative role they play in 'othering' the stranger.
- Reflect on how social conditioning influences our thinking and behaviour.
- Consider different psychology experiments and their relevance to EDI.

Fear

Fear can be thought of as both rational and irrational. It would be rational to fear an apex predator like a wild large cat that could cause us grievous bodily harm. But is it rational to fear a spider that we know cannot harm us? Claustrophobia – a fear of enclosed spaces, or acrophobia – a fear of heights are examples of fears that might be considered rational. Spheksophobia is the fear of wasps, which you could argue is rational because they can sting you, but people's reactions can be disproportionate, given that a sting only causes some discomfort for a few days and the number of people who die from anaphylaxis from a sting is very, very low.

The point is, no child is born afraid. Instead, they learn to be fearful. To keep them safe, we warn them against things like stranger danger, introducing the idea that people they don't know could be a threat. This fear is embedded further through the stories they are told, like the three little pigs, or Little Red

Riding Hood. In both, the threat is the Big Bad Wolf (who incidentally happens to be depicted as black, brown or grey and never white, therefore, carrying possible racial undertones). Side note: Goldilocks, a blue-eyed, blonde, white girl, who trespasses, breaks property, steals food and occupies the three bears' home, is never depicted as the villain of the story. Why is that?

This concept of 'fearing the stranger' and the idea that anyone different from us is a potential threat, is all a part of our survival instinct. This may well have served a purpose historically, but in the present day, it prevents us from connecting to others and seeing them as equals.

It is also misleading to assume that danger comes primarily from strangers, when many cases of child abuse are perpetrated by someone the child knows and who has access to them. It is better to teach the child about people danger or strange behaviours, such as inappropriate words or actions they need to be wary of. A child who sees all strangers as a threat will not be able to ask for help from a stranger, even when that stranger is a paramedic or a police officer, simply because they fall into the category of being someone unknown. Creating irrational fears is just one part of our social conditioning.

> **KEY POINT**
>
> Everyone has fears. Some of these are rational. Others are less so.

Social conditioning and childhood influences

Children learn a lot in the playground. Gender roles, group dynamics and social behaviour all come to the fore at playtime, and children internalize everything they observe.

This has been happening for years. In the 1970s, westerns were still on the TV set in the wild west. The messaging, intended or not, was that the good guys were the cowboys and the bad guys were typically the native Americans, who were often depicted as barbaric, attacking and encircling the cowboys' wagon trains, forcing the cowboys to defend themselves. This is the same tired narrative that is rolled out by colonial settlers throughout history to date. Or if the bad guys were other cowboys, then the good guys were shown as the ones in white, while the bad ones wore black. In schools everywhere, children would recreate what they had seen, playing 'Cowboys and Indians', with everyone wanting to be a cowboy and nobody wanting to be the 'Indians'.

Another game that has been played in playgrounds for decades is 'doctors and nurses', with boys being the doctors and girls playing the nurses, because again, when going to the GP or hospital, that is what children saw, particularly in the 1970s and 1980s. While this is certainly starting to shift, with many more female doctors in the workplace and this likely being reflected in the playground, consider how you answered the riddle in Chapter 3. Did you assume the doctor was a man? An internet search for fancy dress costumes consistently yields the same results. In every instance, whether looking at adults' or children's costumes, the doctor's costume is worn by a male, and a female wears the nurse's costume. With few exceptions, the nurse's adult outfits are usually revealing and sexualized, revealing the inherent misogyny.

This normalization among children, sets the foundations for us as adults.

STOP AND THINK

Do you have any irrational fears about marginalized groups of people? How has your childhood shaped your views of others?

The 'white saviour' narrative

Muhammad Ali, the boxing legend, called out social conditioning during an interview with chat show host, Michael Parkinson back in 1971.[2] In it, he questioned the positive association with the colour white, and the negative connotations with the colour black. Ali pointed out that Jesus, Mary, his followers, the Pope and the Holy Angels were all supposedly white, so Ali joked that this must mean the Black angels were in the kitchen preparing the milk and honey. He questioned why Tarzan, a white man, was beating up the local Africans, was the King of the Jungle, and able to speak with the animals, while the Africans, having been there for centuries, couldn't do the same. He noted that the President lived in the White House, Mary had a little lamb with feet as white as snow, Snow White and Santa Claus were white.

Ali observed the way that everything bad was black. The little, ugly duckling was the black duck, and the black cat meant bad luck, there was blackmail, but no whitemail. It was a humorous interview, but clearly demonstrates the importance of words and how they can be used to convey certain associations, which is not surprising, given the colonial history.

It was also over 50 years ago. Has much changed? We still tell our children stories about the ugly duckling – the black duck who is unwanted and unwelcomed by the other farmyard animals until the duckling transforms into a beautiful, white swan. The messaging, intended or not, is quite blatant regarding what is being defined as beauty. In 2017, the cosmetic brand Dove apologized for a Facebook advertising campaign in which a Black woman removed her T-shirt to reveal a white woman underneath. While this was likely intended to represent diversity, many interpreted it as a Black woman being cleansed into whiteness.

As Ali noted, Jesus and Mary are usually depicted as white, blonde and blue-eyed, despite originating from Bethlehem, which means they are most likely to have had dark skin, brown eyes and black hair. Their images have been 'whitewashed'. Jesus, as the White male saviour is a damaging, misleading trope still played out in Hollywood, with the title lead actor, typically a white male, literally saving the day, as seen in films like *The Great Wall* starring Matt Damon as the white male lead who saves China. In the film, the Chinese just cannot work out how to beat their enemy until Matt Damon's character, William, comes along.

KEY POINT

The 'white saviour' narrative reinforces white supremacy and inferiority complexes for People of Colour.

Psychology experiments

Since the 1940s, several experiments have been conducted which give us insight into social conditioning, especially in relation to EDI. They expose how discrimination emerges from social conditioning, implicit biases, group identity, authority pressures and dehumanization. Some of these are presented below in chronological order. It's worth noting that many of these would be considered unethical today because of their lasting impact on participants, but, nonetheless, they are very revealing.

The Doll Test 1940s

Black civil rights activists and doctors, Kenneth and Mamie Clark, used dolls to test children's understanding of race.[3] The children were African American between the ages of three to seven. They were asked to identify the race of the dolls, which were completely identical except that one was a white doll with blonde hair, and the other doll was brown with black hair. The children were asked to select the doll they preferred through a series of questions like, 'Which doll would you play with?', 'Which one is the nice doll?', 'Which one looks bad?', 'Which one has the nicer colour?', and other questions.

Significantly, the children preferred the white doll and attributed positive associations with the doll. The findings concluded that 'prejudice, discrimination and segregation' created a feeling of inferiority among African American children and damaged their self-esteem.

The Clarks' work helped contribute to a US Supreme Court ruling that racial segregation in public education was unconstitutional.

The Doll Test has been repeated many times since the 1940s, with the results consistently showing that children have a bias, in favour of the white doll. The Doll Test underscores how even young children understand racism – that being white is favourable and favoured by society.

Asch Conformity Experiment 1951

Solomon Asch wanted to understand whether peer pressure could influence a person to conform with the wider group. The experiment involved a group of participants being asked to match the length of lines on cards, with there being a clear right and wrong answer.[4]

Only one person from the group, the 'test subject', was a real participant, but this is not something they were aware of, believing the others were all genuine test subjects.

The other participants answered first, and the test subject answered last. Initially the whole group gave correct answers but later, the fake participants deliberately opted for an incorrect answer. This left the test subject with the option to give the correct answer, thereby going against the majority and being notably different from the group, or to knowingly offer the incorrect answer, thereby conforming to the group.

Most test subjects gave incorrect answers, explaining that while they did not believe in their answers, they had opted to align with the group out of fear of being ridiculed or regarded as strange. A few test subjects became convinced that the wider group's answers were correct.

> **KEY POINT**
>
> In the workplace, conforming means not being your authentic self, due to a desire to be included. Conforming can also contribute to discriminatory practices. A person may participate in racist 'banter' among peers, knowing it is wrong and not something they would do outside of work, but they do it anyway, to 'fit in'.

For more on conforming, refer to Chapter 2 'Authenticity versus conforming', Chapter 3 'Conformity bias' and Chapter 6 'Diverse recruitment panels'.

> **KEY POINT**
>
> People conform because they want to fit in (normative influence) or because they believe the group knows best (informational influence).

The Robbers Cave Experiment and the Contact Hypothesis 1954

Muzafer Sherif studied intergroup conflict and cooperation among 22 12-year-old boys at Robber's Cave State Park, Oklahoma, America.[5] The boys were white, middle-class, Protestant and from a two-parent household. None of the boys knew each other before the study.

The boys were evenly divided into two groups with balanced physical, mental and social skills. Neither group was aware of the other's existence. Each group developed their own identity and bonded over activities during a period of five to six days.

The groups were introduced to each other and competed for the next four to six days, with prizes awarded to the winners. This led to increasing hostility between the two groups, with the researchers physically separating them because they had become so hostile towards each other.

Later, for a period of six to seven days, cooperative tasks were introduced, requiring the two groups to work together, which reduced conflict.

Some of the key findings were:

- When there is a resource scarcity and some form of competition, it can lead to hostility.
- Groups can develop an intense sense of 'us and them', an 'ingroup' and 'outgroup', leading to prejudice towards the other group.
- Hostility between groups of people can be reduced through having shared goals to collaborate on.

KEY POINT

In the workplace, if diverse groups are isolated from each other, there is a risk of developing division and friction, but this can be addressed through having shared objectives and activities to work on collaboratively.

These findings were underscored by another psychology experiment carried out by Gordon Allport, known as the Contact Hypothesis.[6] Allport found that positive interactions between ingroups and outgroups enable more positive perceptions and fewer negative perceptions of that outgroup.

The study was initially centred on racial differences, but has been found to be applicable between ingroup-outgroup relations across religion, age, sexuality, economic circumstances etc. There are some conditions for this approach to be successful, which include the absence of hierarchical status, sharing a common goal and having a non-competitive environment.

Notably in 2017, Google's 'DeepMind'[7] had AI agents compete against each other in a virtual game, with each AI agent collecting as many apples as possible. They had the option of temporarily eliminating their opponent from the game by shooting them with a laser beam. If there were a sufficient number of apples, it was fine but once the apples were in short supply, the AI agents became aggressive, targeting each other and emulating human, negative traits. However, if a benefit was introduced, then the AI agents were able to work collaboratively.

KEY POINT

Having positive interactions with those we see as different helps break down barriers, resists an 'us and them' mindset and frees us from our own echo chambers.

STOP AND THINK

Are there any 'in and out' groups in your workplace that are unhelpful?

The Milgram Experiment 1961

Stanley Milgram conducted an experiment focusing on the conflict between obedience to authority and personal conscience.[8] He was trying to understand the defence put forward by those accused of genocide during World War II, at the Nuremberg

War Criminal trials, who claimed that they were just following orders from their superiors.

Person A was the only real test subject of the experiment, and Person B and C were both acting, aware of the real intent behind the experiment.

Person B was given a memory test, and each time they made a mistake, Person A was asked to administer an 'electric shock' to Person B, on the authority of Person C. The 'voltage' of the shock was consecutively increased for each incorrect answer.

There was no actual electric shock, but Person B would fake a reaction, convincing Person A they were experiencing pain. If Person A refused to administer the shock at any point, then Person C would give several firm directions to persuade Person A to continue.

Test subjects A exhibited signs of stress: sweating, biting their lips, trembling, stuttering, digging nails into their flesh, and nervous laughter. But alarmingly, all administered 'electric shocks' up to 300 volts, with 65 per cent continuing to the upper limit of 450 volts.

Milgram found that ordinary people are likely to obey an authority figure, potentially causing harm to others, since the instructions are coming from an external source, so the responsibility can be passed on to them. Although, this doesn't stop the individual from experiencing significant stress and anxiety.

Later, studies found that people were less likely to obey harmful orders when they saw others resist, demonstrating how collective action can counteract discrimination and mistreatment.

KEY POINT

In the workplace, the Milgram experiment may explain why others can become part of systemic discrimination and cruelty, by not questioning someone in a position of authority and allowing the abuse to continue.

Learned helplessness 1967

Martin Seligman and Steven F Maier, American psychologists, were researching depression through experimenting with the response displayed by dogs.[9]

One of the experiments involved administering low-level electric shocks to a dog. Dog A could end the shock by pressing a lever, however, for Dog B, the lever had no effect, so the shock was unavoidable. A second experiment was carried out in in an enclosed space with a low barrier between the two halves of the chamber. Both dogs could escape the electric shock by jumping over the barrier to the other side where there would be no shock. Dog A jumped to the other side, but Dog B lay there passively and whined, accepting that there was nothing that could be done to escape the shock. This was the result of learned helplessness.

Learned helplessness can leave the victim feeling a loss of control and accepting that the situation is not going to get better, so that they stop objecting to discrimination, allowing it to normalize.

KEY POINT

In the workplace, victims of discrimination can develop learned helplessness. This can occur after a victim has tried to confront the 'abuser' or has reported them to their line manager or HR, but nothing changes, and the abuse continues.

Learned helplessness may explain why marginalized individuals do not put themselves forward for promotional opportunities because experience has taught them that people like themselves will not be successful.

The Blue Eyes/Brown Eyes Experiment 1968

The day after Martin Luther King Jr was shot, Jane Elliott, a US school teacher, devised an experiment to teach her 'all white' class about racism.[10] She divided the class between those with blue eyes and brown eyes, as Hitler's decision on who was going to the gas chamber was partially linked to eye colour.

The blue-eyed children were told they were 'superior, smarter and more well-behaved' than the children with brown eyes and were given special privileges like longer break times. The brown-eyed children had to wear armbands to signify they were brown-eyed, and if they made a mistake, this was attributed to their eye colour. Elliot also reversed the experiment, making the blue-eyed children wear the arm band and making them feel inferior. In each case, the superior group had the support of the authoritative figure, in this case, Elliot, as the teacher.

The superior group acted arrogantly and would tease the inferior group, while the inferior group increasingly became withdrawn. At break times, there were even violent interactions, even though before the experiment, the children had all been friends.

The children were all given the same spelling and maths tests, and the children who had been told they were superior performed better than those who had been labelled as inferior, thus becoming a self-fulfilling prophecy.

In a separate address to a room full of white adults, Elliot asked every white person in the room to stand up if they would be happy to be treated as Black citizens were treated in society. No one stood up. Elliot continued, 'Nobody's standing here. That says very plainly that you know what's happening, you know you don't want it for you. I want to know why you're so willing to accept it or to allow it to happen for others.'

Elliot was calling out the audience's wilful blindness (refer to Chapter 2). The Doll Test highlighted how we become aware of inequities in society during childhood, and as adults, we can fail to address these injustices.

> **KEY POINT**
>
> In the workplace, a lack of equity results in one group being
> favoured, rewarded and their performance boosted, due to a
> belief in superiority and institutional support. However, this is to
> the detriment of others.

The Bystander Effect 1968

'The bystander effect' experiment was first conducted by
psychologists, John Darley and Bibb Latané in 1968, following
the highly publicized murder of Kitty Genovese in New York.[11]
She was chased by her assailant and stabbed repeatedly and
sexually assaulted, during an attack lasting over half an hour.
Genovese called for help, and out of 38 neighbours who were
aware of the attack, no one responded.

The experiment sought to understand why people had such
apathy, which might also explain why nothing was done to stop
the rise of fascism in Germany, a question still relevant in parts
of the world right now.

The test subjects were exposed to a situation of increasing
severity, and it was consistently found that if the test subject was
alone, then they were likely to intervene. However, if they were
in the room with just one other person, then the response rate
fell dramatically.

So, for example, in one scenario, the test subject A was talking to actor B over an intercom, and the actor B pretended to
have a seizure, making choking sounds and saying they were
going to die. If the test subject A was alone, within a single
minute, 85 per cent tried to check on person B. However, if test
subject A was with another individual, person C, and person C
did not respond, then only 31 per cent responded after 3 minutes.

Studies found that if a bystander sees that other witnesses are
doing nothing, then he or she will also do nothing and the

greater the number of bystanders, the less likely any one of them is to help, due to a diffusion of personal responsibility.

> KEY POINT
>
> In the workplace, the bystander effect may explain why nobody acts when inappropriate behaviour occurs, leading to a toxic and discriminatory culture.

The Minimal Group Paradigm and Social Identity Theory Experiments 1970s

Henri Tajfel, a Polish Jew, who had lost family members during World War II, wanted to understand how genocide is possible (a question still relevant today) by exploring what minimal conditions were required for discrimination to occur between different groups.

One of the experiments involved dividing a group of 48 school children, according to their preference for abstract paintings, one painted by Paul Klee and the other by Wassily Kandinsky.[12] Another group allocation was on the arbitrary flip of a coin.

The studies found that people favour their own ingroup, while showing prejudice towards the other group, even when those divisions are meaningless. This helps to explain why the 'us and them' rivalry exists between schools located in the same geographical area or between sports fans, loyal to their declared team and vitriol towards other teams. At a societal level, it may contribute to nationalism and populism.

> KEY POINT
>
> In workplaces, this behaviour can manifest along hierarchical and functional divides, or be directed towards certain groups.

> **TOP TIP**
> Mitigate divisions through project teams
>
> Project teams working across the hierarchy and functional structures, helping to bring together different parts of the organization by creating a shared purpose, can help to mitigate against artificial divisions.

The Stanford Prison Experiment 1971

Psychology professor, Philip Zimbardo, conducted what would become a controversial experiment, in trying to understand whether a situation made people act the way they do, rather than their disposition.[13] Twenty-four test subjects, all white middle-class males, appearing mentally stable, were selected and randomly assigned either the role of prisoners or prison guards.

The prison guards were given prison uniforms to remove their individuality; wearing mirrored sunglasses to prevent eye contact and carrying wooden batons, but were specifically told not to physically hurt the prisoners, nor deny them food or drink. The local police arrested the 'prisoners' at home, without warning, and took them through the full process to make the simulation feel more authentic, finally placing them in small holding cells. The prison guards referred to the prisoners by their prison number, rather than their name, to remove individuality.

Intended to last two weeks, the experiment was forced to end after only six days. Even though they all knew it was meant to be a simulation, the prison guards began behaving increasingly sadistically, inflicting humiliation and suffering on the prisoners who became subservient, allowing themselves to be dehumanized and showing extreme stress and depression. Worryingly, the guards enjoyed the power they wielded, yet none of the preliminary tests were able to predict this behaviour.

KEY POINT

In hierarchical organizations, senior leaders can potentially abuse their power, (refer to Chapter 7, 'Power imbalance'), negatively impacting junior staff who can become compliant due to learned helplessness. This can foster a toxic and discriminatory culture. Flatter structures, where leadership is more equally distributed, can help limit the abuse of power.

WHAT WOULD YOU DO?
Number 4

The sales team, who are mostly white, regard themselves as the most important part of the business. They hold the view that other parts of the business are inferior, particularly the logistics and transportation team, which primarily consists of Black, Asian and Eastern European low-skilled workers. This can lead to some heated interactions.

- What are the concerns with this division between the teams?
- What actions could you take to encourage collaboration and greater cohesion?

CHAPTER SUMMARY

- We have developed fears through our own lived experience and societal factors that can prevent us from seeing all people equally.
- From childhood to adulthood, we have been socially conditioned to think and behave in a particular way that is unhelpful.
- Psychology experiments help us understand why we behave in a certain way and how this can manifest in the workplace.

REVIEW QUESTIONS

1 Name three ways that children could be affected by social conditioning in the playground.

2 What is learned helplessness and how can it manifest in the workplace?

3 Explain the bystander effect and how it can manifest in the workplace.

Endnotes

1 Liddle, D (2021) *Transformational Culture*, Kogan Page

2 https://www.bbc.co.uk/news/av/world-us-canada-52988605 (archived at https://perma.cc/P4Y9-RDLB)

3 https://kennethclark.commons.gc.cuny.edu/the-doll-study/ (archived at https://perma.cc/4YG7-MLNC)

4 https://www.simplypsychology.org/asch-conformity.html (archived at https://perma.cc/29NH-W7C5)

5 https://www.simplypsychology.org/robbers-cave.html (archived at https://perma.cc/659K-RJBX)

6 https://www.simplypsychology.org/contact-hypothesis.html (archived at https://perma.cc/J2M8-WLV7)

7 https://www.zmescience.com/science/news-science/google-deepmind-aggressiveness/ (archived at https://perma.cc/Q6J8-89ER)

8 https://www.simplypsychology.org/milgram.html (archived at https://perma.cc/GM5F-ALDP)

9 https://www.simplypsychology.org/learned-helplessness.html (archived at https://perma.cc/ZHZ2-LZ68)

10 https://practicalpie.com/blue-eyes-brown-eyes-jane-elliott/ (archived at https://perma.cc/27MU-CCKL)

11 https://www.simplypsychology.org/bystander-effect.html (archived at https://perma.cc/D3ZJ-QGBM)

12 https://psychologyfanatic.com/the-minimal-group-paradigm/ (archived at https://perma.cc/MD9P-8XGF)
13 https://www.simplypsychology.org/zimbardo.html (archived at https://perma.cc/YCG6-ZC56)

CHAPTER FIVE

EDI initiatives

Introduction

What do EDI initiatives mean to you? Training? Policies? Something else?

EDI initiatives vary between organizations, with many adopting what they see as 'best practice'. However, best practice does not always mean addressing inequalities – it's often more effective to focus on a 'best fit' approach with tailored offerings to suit specific organizational needs. Every organization has different leadership, resources and challenges – even similar organizations in the same industry – so a one-size-fits-all approach rarely works.

Success depends on leadership's appetite for genuine EDI progress. Without real commitment, even the best EDI strategy will struggle to gain traction. That's where you come in – supporting this journey to identify necessary EDI initiatives and building a business case for them (which we'll explore further in Chapter 8).

This chapter explores some of the most common EDI initiatives, highlighting their benefits and potential pitfalls.

LEARNING OBJECTIVES

By the end of this chapter, you will be able to:

- Identify and explain some of the most widely used EDI initiatives.
- Understand how these initiatives contribute to an inclusive workplace.
- Evaluate the effectiveness of these EDI initiatives in driving change.
- Be able to recommend EDI initiatives for your organization.

EDI training

EDI training is the most common EDI initiative in organizations. But what does it entail? It's not a straightforward question to answer, and it very much depends on the organization.

While EDI training helps create greater awareness and understanding, it doesn't necessarily lead to any meaningful, lasting change, unless done in conjunction with other activities.

The position EDI occupies in an organization will partially determine the approach to the EDI training. If EDI has been bought into by the senior leadership team, then EDI training is usually mandated to take place at the start of employment, followed by an annual refresher. If EDI doesn't have leadership buy-in, it can just be a one-off event, which has limited impact.

Like with most things, you get what you pay for. Some organizations opt for low-cost, off-the-shelf options, which will typically involve online training provided by an EDI consultancy. This training may involve information being shared through examples, case studies and videos, followed by multiple-choice questions to check understanding.

Often this is mandated training, taking a 'sheep-dip approach'. This has the advantage of every single staff member receiving the same level of training, which would also assist in defending the organization from a tribunal claim. The disadvantage is that this type of training can be regarded as a tick-box exercise by the trainees, feeling that the employer has not sufficiently invested in the employee, with actions failing to reflect the declared commitment to EDI.

Sheep-dip approach: A one-size-fits-all, ineffective approach to training that has limited application to or impact on employees' daily work.

For senior leaders, more in-depth training is required as they are legally responsible for their workforce, so they need to be a role model to others. Ideally, this training needs to be live training, whether face-to-face or video conferencing, to encourage questions and challenges in a safe space, where no questions are off limits and leaders can be vulnerable.

The time allocated to train leaders is indicative of how seriously they have committed themselves to an inclusive culture. For example, a two-hour training session is unlikely to allow enough time for discussion, debate and self-reflection.

TOP TIP
Allow enough time for leadership EDI training

EDI training for senior leaders should take a minimum of a day. This allows the pace to be slower and creates space for honest and robust conversations.

Training content

For some organizations, EDI training entails an introduction to the Equality Act 2010, the nine protected characteristics, possibly unconscious bias training and/or cultural competency. But the actual make-up of the training will vary depending on the content or modules selected from a training provider. Sometimes, EDI training will have a particular focus to address specific issues arising in the workplace, such as sexism or racism.

EXERCISE

Do you know what EDI training your organization currently offers? If not, do some research to find out. Based on what you've learned in this section, are there any areas that could be improved?

Targeted interventions and positive action

It's common for organizations to be aware that despite having diversity in their business, certain marginalized groups are not progressing in their careers. This can be due to a combination of reasons, such as a lack of confidence, relevant experience and required qualifications. Lack of confidence could arise from:

- Not seeing representation in senior roles.
- Having a lack of faith in the robustness of the recruitment process.
- Being a returner to the workplace after a career break.
- Having low self-esteem due to an inferiority complex.
- Past experiences (learned helplessness).

Lack of relevant experience can make securing a senior role qualification difficult, while the lack of qualifications could relate to social mobility. Whatever the reasons are, a targeted intervention could directly address these barriers through positive action (refer to Chapter 1 for a definition of positive action).

All of these approaches can be impactful in supporting a person from a marginalized group in their career progression. However, if those opportunities don't exist due to a flat structure and low staff turnover, or worse, if employees are still overlooked despite being suited, then it can be counter-productive, leading to cynicism and a growing belief that these interventions are tick-box initiatives only.

There are different targeted interventions to consider depending on the barrier to progression, ranging from structured training to less formal approaches.

Development for diverse applicants

Internal diverse applicants are sometimes rejected at the shortlisting stage because they lack the relevant qualifications: technical and/or people skills.

Regular development conversations can help to understand career aspirations and ensure that internal applicants are supported to meet any shortfall in their formal qualifications and skillsets. This will help to put them on equal footing with other internal applicants in progressing to the shortlisting stage.

TOP TIP
See training as an investment

Formal training can be expensive, but adopt a longer-term view and see it as an investment, not just a cost. Safeguards can be built into training contracts, such as requiring the trainee to commit to a reasonable length of service, so that there is a return on investment on the training and development.

Buddying

Being new in any organization or group setting is hard enough. Being from a marginalized group can amplify any feelings of isolation.

For any 'newbie', it can be difficult to approach a line manager, especially about something already explained previously. Given the number of issues a new starter must contend with, from people, processes and policies to physical locations etc., it can be overwhelming and leave a person feeling lost. This is where having an informal buddy can be helpful, where the 'buddy' is at the same or similar level, without any line management relationship and who can support and sense check understanding.

Having a 'buddy' appointed allows the new person time to find their feet, become familiar with the culture and make social relations, which in turn enables the new starter to focus on the work and increases the likelihood of a successful appointment and longer-term retention.

The buddy does not need to have the same lived experience, but it can be an advantage to have someone to relate to, especially if they are at a similar level within the hierarchy.

STOP AND THINK

Does a buddying system exist in your organization? If not, what would you need to do to set one up?

Mentoring (and reverse mentoring)

A mentor is usually someone who is an expert in their field, having already undergone the career journey which the mentee aspires to, and is therefore well placed to advise a mentee in a more senior or challenging role. One advantage of having a mentor is that the mentee avoids some of the pitfalls and mistakes the mentor has made in their past, thereby, receiving the gift of hindsight. Note that mentoring is intended to be 'handholding', rather than 'spoon feeding'.

Having a mentor can be an invaluable resource to enable someone to fast-track their learning journey, but there needs to be clarity on the mentor's role and expectations of the mentee.

(Good) mentoring occurs through a formal relationship and establishes agreed-upon touchpoints or a number of hours of support. A mentor can be appointed to advise and recommend certain actions or support the mentee with work challenges and issues.

Finding a mentor who might have a similar lived experience to the mentee is more challenging if there is a lack of diversity in senior roles, and could cause a gap in understanding the mentee's perspective. Some organizations lean into this disparity, with an expectation of reciprocation, whereby the mentor mentors the mentee, but also vice versa. This is referred to as reverse mentoring and means that both parties are developing differently.

TOP TIP
Look for opportunities for reverse mentoring

Reverse mentoring can be extremely beneficial and empowering for mentees. If finding a mentor with a similar lived experience as a mentee is difficult, look for opportunities for reverse mentoring.

Coaching

A coach does not necessarily need to be an expert in the same field as the person they are coaching. The coach's core contribution is not offering solutions and advice. It is about asking the right questions and letting the coachee find their own answers, which will not always mean the right answer, but accepting that is part of the learning journey. Having a coach can help the coachee with their self-directed learning by challenging their thinking and actions.

When asked the question, 'What should I do in this situation?', a good coach will respond with more questions, for example: 'What do *you* think you should do in this situation?',

'What have you tried already?' or 'What are your options?', but not dive in with an actual answer.

(Good) coaching, like mentoring, is usually done through a formal relationship and agreed touchpoints, or a number of hours for support.

KEY POINTS

The terms 'mentoring' and 'coaching' are sometimes used interchangeably, but they are distinct and different.

Shadowing

Shadowing someone in a more senior post can expose a person from a marginalized group to the context, culture and practices involved in that role. It allows a person to understand the required mindset and thinking process, effectively 'walking in the other person's shoes', therefore, complementing theoretical training and development.

Shadowing can help to demystify senior roles and spaces, making them more accessible and attainable, while also providing increased networking opportunities, which may lead to mentoring opportunities.

This can all be very helpful when there is an experience gap, so when the opportunity arises to apply for the role, the applicant is better placed to be successful.

One of the biggest challenges with shadowing is time constraints and finding available opportunities, because it will have an impact on the work schedule of a senior person, who needs to fully appreciate the value of the person shadowing them.

Shadowing can mean being fully immersed in the same area of work to appreciate the fullness of the role, but it can also be selective, such as attending only certain meetings as an observer, giving insights into how points are articulated and how decisions are made.

> **STOP AND THINK**
>
> Does shadowing occur in your organization? If not, would any
> barriers need to be overcome to make it possible?

Policies

Policies are useful to clarify practices and behaviours in an
organization when delivering the stated objectives. They are not
usually written with an EDI lens, and so don't consider whether
they are inclusive, supportive and welcoming to those who are
different.

Whether or not certain policies are included or not can signal
an organization's dedication to fostering a fair, inclusive and
supportive environment for all employees.

There are some obvious policies clearly related to EDI, such
as those listed below. It should be pointed out; this is not
intended to be a complete list but rather is indicative of more
well-known policies.

- **Code of Conduct** embeds respect, dignity and inclusion in
  workplace interactions, promoting accountability.

- **Equal Opportunity Policy** outlines the organization's commitment to ensuring equal treatment in hiring, promotion,
  training and all employment practices.

- **Anti-Discrimination Policy** prohibits discrimination based
  on race, gender, age, disability, sexual orientation, religion or
  other protected characteristics.

- **Bullying and Harassment Policy** defines unacceptable
  behaviours, establishes reporting procedures and outlines
  consequences for violations.

- **Flexible Working Policy** supports work–life balance by offering flexible hours, remote work options and job-sharing opportunities.

- **Family-Friendly Policies** includes parental leave, adoption leave and support for caregivers to foster inclusion for employees with family responsibilities.

- **Reasonable Adjustments Policy** provides accommodations for employees with disabilities, ensuring equitable access to work environments and opportunities.

- **Recruitment Policy** can focus on attracting diverse candidates and mitigating unconscious bias in hiring processes.

- **Training and Development Policy** can mandate training in areas like unconscious bias, cultural competence and inclusive leadership.

- **Pay Equity Policy** helps to ensures equitable compensation regardless of gender, ethnicity or other characteristics.

- **Whistleblowing Policy** encourages employees to report concerns without fear of retaliation.

- **Health and Safety Policy** can ensure diverse wellbeing needs are met and catered for, such as workplace adjustments for disabilities and establishing places for worship and contemplation.

- **Menopause policy** supports women in the workplace going through menopause and create awareness for better understanding from line managers and colleagues.

- **Transition Policy** supports an employee's transition by clarifying how HR can assist with a transition plan which could include communication preferences, workplace adjustments and timelines for changes.

> **EXERCISE**
>
> How many of these policies do you have in your organization?
> List those that you have and highlight any gaps.

Employee Resource Groups

Employee Resource Groups (ERGs) are sometimes known as Employee Network Groups or Affinity Groups.

The first ERG was for Black employees in 1964 launched by Xerox during the civil rights riots in New York.[1] Since then, ERGs have become widespread across every industry and sector.

ERGs are typically set up in larger organizations, but not exclusively. They are platforms for people with a shared affinity for an area or identity coming together periodically to share information, resources, ideas and experiences.

ERGs often form organically around shared identities or experiences to support EDI efforts, but can differ in terms of mandate. They can have loose membership and be open to others, allies and champions who don't share the same affinity or identity, or they can be closed to ensure it is a safe space for those attending.

Common ERGs include specific groups for women, race, disability and LGBTQ+, but larger organizations often have more for other areas of difference, and not just the protected characteristics, e.g. working parents, socioeconomic class, faith, veterans and ex-offenders.

The role of an ERG can be limited to a platform for like-minded individuals, and can risk becoming a 'moan and groan session'. Another downside can be that the ERG is 'preaching to the choir', engaging with those internally who already know and understand the issues, rather than the wider work population. ERGs with no clear mandate, that are under-resourced and expected to run sessions in the members' own time, can become forums for cynicism which negates any actual gains.

However, ERGs with clear terms of reference, sponsorship from an executive leader and the time and budget to hold meetings and carry out activities can have a visible impact. They can be used as a sounding board to review new policies or support recruitment panels, to ensure visible representation of diversity.

Simple mistakes can undermine an ERG. For example, asking an 'ERG for race' what they want to see happen during Black History Month, a mere week before the month is due to start would send a clear message to all the members that you are not taking them seriously and are just seeing the ERG as a tick-box exercise. Similarly, asking the ERGs to solve the problems they are suffering from, that they aren't responsible for creating, is unlikely to be received well. ERG members have lived experience, but not necessarily the skills or authority to bring about real change. An ERG can be part of the solution, for example, by contributing their viewpoints, but they are not *the* solution.

TOP TIP
Coordinate and collaborate

ERGs that coordinate and collaborate can accelerate their efforts through shared resources and learning from one another, i.e. having the chairs of all ERGs meet periodically as part of an EDI council.

Allyship

In principle, being an ally should be straightforward. An ally is like a friend. They show up when you need them and are in your corner. You can rely on them and turn to them for support. In the workplace, allyship is everything you would expect from a friend, within professional boundaries.

Allyship: The active, consistent and intentional practice of supporting and advocating for marginalized groups and educating others.

Allyship goes beyond passive support; in other words, not being the type of person who comes to you after the incident and tells you they believe you were right, but did not speak up in the moment. Allies are often workplace champions, there to amplify the voices of minorities and typically, they do not have the protected characteristic they champion.

An ally will often use their position of influence or their privilege to be effective advocates in challenging discrimination, amplifying underrepresented voices, and pushing for meaningful change. This is why having a senior leader champion a particular employee resource group or event can be impactful in raising awareness and encouraging participation, by using their hierarchical power.

With allyship, it is not necessarily about doing the big things, but rather, it can be the small daily interactions that end up having the greatest, sustainable impact.

For example, a white colleague notices that a Black co-worker's (X) ideas are being dismissed in a meeting, so they opt to speak up and say, 'I think X raised a great point earlier, which needs exploring further', thus attributing the idea to that person and ensuring everyone is reminded of that fact.

Another example could involve a straight friend correcting someone who makes an inappropriate joke about LGBTQ+ people, reminding the person, 'That's not funny. Let's be respectful.'

Being an ally requires one to be brave, as they are standing up for others, which might put a 'target on their back', hence why allies in senior roles can be more effective. This is because they are afforded a degree of protection, in comparison to someone else more junior in the hierarchy, or someone in an insecure role, such as a fixed-term contract.

> **KEY POINT**
>
> Allyship is not about being a saviour. It's about listening, learning and acting in a way that empowers others.

Diversity calendar

Diversity calendars can be useful to ensure certain key dates are not missed throughout the year, and are not just noted, but celebrated and can even be part of an awareness programme.

Typically, a diversity calendar will highlight key religious days, including birthdays of religious leaders, cultural celebrations, special events, anniversaries, festivals and internationally recognized and UN-mandated days, in addition to the usual bank holidays.

Bringing a focus to these dates helps to foster a sense of inclusion because marginalized groups feel both seen and heard. Events can promote greater awareness and discourse around differences.

An EDI calendar marks global dates such as Martin Luther King Junior Day, Holocaust Memorial Day and International Women's Day, or UK-specific dates, like Windrush Day and Stephen Lawrence Day. Other dates include religious festivals, such as Easter, Christmas, Holi and Diwali (Hinduism), Passover and Yom Kippur (Judaism) and Ramadan, Eid ul Fitr and Eid ul Haj (Islam). Some events last several days such as Deaf Awareness Week or Race Equality Week, while other events are a month long, such as Women's History, LGBT+ Pride, Black History and Ramadan.

> **TOP TIP**
> Find a diversity calendar
>
> Diversity calendars are produced by CIPD, EDI consultancies and others, some of which are freely available, but nevertheless, all will have some similarities and differences as there are so many potential dates throughout the year to commemorate or take note of. Even reading the events listed above will have you asking the question, what about X or Y?

Fireside chats

A fireside chat conjures up an image of someone sat in an armchair, wearing a night gown and slippers, in front of a blazing fire in the living room, with the family pet at their feet. It is a very relaxed and intimate setting, where a person feels comfortable sharing some unique perspectives with others in a non-threatening, safe space.

Fireside chats can be great for fostering authentic conversations and recruiting allies. They can be part of the diversity calendar, bringing a focus to a specific issue of difference during the year.

Typically, a fireside chat is a moderated conversation between the host and a guest and involves the guest sharing their lived experience with others, generating empathy and a shared connection. Fireside chats can be quite raw and unscripted, which can lead to tangents or triggering other attendees.

Fireside chats can be delivered internally or by an external outsider, and there are advantages and disadvantages to both options. Internal speakers can be great in that they are more relatable as they are already known to their colleagues, and if it is a senior leader, it can be a great opportunity to build trust by showing vulnerability and appearing more human. However, the internal person then has to continue in the organization and may feel more self-conscious after having bared their souls. There is also a risk they will not be able to handle challenging questions from attendees, which is where the moderator's role is so critical.

An external person, like an EDI consultant, can sow seeds and be part of creating awareness and is more likely to have encountered challenging questions if this is part of the services they offer to organizations. External guests can be expensive, but may attract a wider range of attendees, thus going beyond 'preaching to the choir'.

Sharing a lived experience can be therapeutic for the person 'opening up', which would normally involve examples of systemic discrimination and barriers faced during their life and career. It can be eye-opening to attendees who have, through their own privilege, never had those life experiences, and who are therefore given the chance to reflect on what it must be like to be different, as well as consider what they can do to be more supportive.

TOP TIP
Be aware of the risks

If the guest makes a controversial or unintended statement, it may present a public relations risk. Be aware of this possibility and manage it to avoid bringing the organization into disrepute.

Pronouns

Pronouns are terms used instead of a person's name. The use of pronouns allows for a person to be referenced according to their preferred gender identity, which may or may not be the same as their biological identity. A person may prefer to be regarded as non-binary or gender non-conforming, meaning neither male nor female, in which case their preferred pronoun is 'they' or 'them'.

Acknowledging a person's preference can be respectful of their lifestyle choice, thus avoiding assumptions and supporting inclusion. Knowing how a person wants to be referred to can enable better working relations with colleagues.

Some employers have added pronouns to their name badges and/or signatures in emails to normalize the usage of pronouns. This practice supports employees of different genders, making them feel included, while preventing the misgendering of others. However, this can risk being seen as virtue signalling, as opposed to being a part of a genuine inclusion effort.

KEY POINT

Misgendering someone can be offensive and could give rise to a discrimination claim.

TOP TIP
Take a 'pronoun sharing' approach

Mandating that everyone declare their preferred pronoun is likely to be met with some resistance for personal, cultural or religious beliefs. Employees may also feel pressured into disclosing their gender identity. Allowing 'pronoun sharing' to be voluntary is a better approach.

Pronunciation of names

An individual's name is a core part of their identity. Most will appreciate someone trying and getting it wrong, rather than not trying at all, as this sends a vastly different message.

LinkedIn introduced a feature allowing a person to record exactly how to pronounce their name, which is a wonderful way to prevent pronunciation mistakes.

A related point to note is the spelling of a person's name. Don't guess, take the time to get it right, as this is a mark of respect.

Rainbows and flags

Many organizations showcase their support for EDI through visible displays on their websites. One of the most visible EDI initiatives is the annual Pride month, which takes place in June. During this month, many organizations liberally use rainbow colours to affirm their commitment to marginalized groups. For example, they may change their branding to rainbow colours.

Similarly, during Black History month, some organizations incorporate black squares or black flags as part of their branding and/or will take a compliance approach, asking staff 'to take a knee', popularized by Colin Kaepernick in 2016 during the NFL games, in support of the Black Lives Matter movement.

These big events are usually in tandem with other 'awareness raising' events, such as conducting fireside chats or inviting guest speakers to talk about a specific strand of difference. These moments can become photo opportunities, later reflected on the organization's website and marketing materials to underscore how inclusive the organization is externally, thereby becoming part of the employer branding and attraction strategy.

TOP TIP

Warning – check for alignment

It can be demotivating for staff if an organization's external messaging is at odds with their lived reality internally. Some regard these activities as performative window dressing if they are done in isolation with no meaningful change to marginalized groups internally.

Workplace culture

Every organization has a culture or subcultures, whether by design or left to grow organically, but how inclusive are they?

Most will have cultural practices, for example, a particular department goes out for drinks on a Friday lunchtime or out on an evening to a local bar to celebrate team successes. Or the culture might be one where everyone is overly familiar with each other, and are 'huggers', or use sexist language that is passed off as banter.

Just in these few examples, multiple marginalized groups could feel excluded or have their personal boundaries crossed to conform. Someone may not want to go out for drinks for religious/personal reasons during the workday or might want to avoid going out on an evening due to caring responsibilities/other family commitments. Moreover, hugging without consent violates personal space and using 'harmless banter', which might be offensive, increases the risk of allegations regarding sexual harassment and discrimination.

To address practices that are not inclusive, you must first understand what cultural practices currently exist in the organization and review them to assess how inclusive and accommodating the environment is. Senior leaders have a vital role to play in shaping the culture, but if they are not diverse themselves, then they may be blindsided to some of the issues.

TOP TIP
Ask your ERGs

To help shape your workplace culture and make it more inclusive, it can be helpful to ask ERGs to share their thoughts and concerns in a safe space.

STOP AND THINK

How inclusive is your organization's culture?

- If you could describe your culture in one sentence, what would you say?
- Name two to three ways that your culture could be more inclusive.
- How effective have EDI initiatives been in creating an inclusive culture?

REAL-WORLD EXAMPLE
Cisco

Cisco's European arm was awarded the top spot on the FT–Statista 2024 list of European Diversity Leaders, decided mostly by employee surveys, and weighted for the experiences of underrepresented groups.

It was able to achieve this through several EDI initiatives, such as leaders taking on roles of allies, mentors and sponsors; offering job swaps to younger employees to boost their experience; training programmes for mid-level women to develop their skills and close the gender gap in leadership.[2]

STOP AND THINK

Does your organization take a 'best practice' or 'best fit' approach to EDI initiatives?

WHAT WOULD YOU DO?
Number 5

Your boss walks in and tells you, 'Our competitors have increased their gender balance by 20 per cent after they introduced mentoring and pronouns on name badges'. She wants you to do the same. Do you agree? What are your options?

CHAPTER SUMMARY

- There are many widely used EDI initiatives which are best practice, but not necessarily best fit.
- These EDI initiatives can contribute to an inclusive workplace.
- EDI initiatives vary in the level of resources they require and may range from a one-off activity to a series of ongoing activities.
- EDI initiatives vary in terms of their impact and effectiveness.

REVIEW QUESTIONS

1 What is the difference between a best practice and best fit approach to EDI initiatives?

2 Name three common policies related to EDI.

3 Name three requirements for ERGs to have a visible impact in the organization.

Endnotes

1 https://www.hrmagazine.co.uk/content/features/back-in-style-the-rise-and-rise-of-employee-led-resource-groups (archived at https://perma.cc/8H52-V4H2)

2 https://www.ft.com/content/58b6b437-69b6-4675-8104-89333b8a6b7e? (archived at https://perma.cc/J26W-NG2L)

CHAPTER SIX

EDI and talent

Introduction

In this chapter, we take the knowledge and understanding from earlier chapters and apply it to how your workplace approaches attracting, recruiting, developing, promoting and remunerating diverse talent. These are some of the main functions of HR and are deeply connected to EDI. Getting them right is crucial to create fair, supportive and inclusive workplaces.

The employee journey starts with attraction and recruitment, which is also where the problem often begins. Candidates are shortlisted and appointed for being a certain fit, based on who they are demographically or who they know, rather than being based on competency and potential. These same individuals are then promoted, often repeatedly for the same reason and rewarded with higher salaries, with processes or policies either lacking or being effectively bypassed to arrive at certain decisions. This results in inequity and an understanding of who is favoured.

This chapter begins by looking at how organizations attract (or fail to attract) diverse talent. We move on to looking at how we need to redefine the talent pool, and consider a broader range of marginalized groups. We progress to considering how we can improve the recruitment process, induction, training, learning and development and remuneration. As you read, keep asking yourself how your organization approaches the different elements of the employee lifecycle we discuss, and where there could be room for improvement.

LEARNING OBJECTIVES

By the end of this chapter, you will be able to:

- Understand how to attract diverse talent in different ways.
- Rethink your understanding of the talent pool.
- Assess the suitability of your recruitment process for diverse talent.
- Understand the barriers faced by diverse talent in accessing training, learning and development.
- Explain the role pay gaps play in surfacing inequity in remuneration.

Attraction

The initial phase of the employee lifecycle – attraction – provides an opportunity for organizations to show that they are serious about attracting and recruiting diverse talent. Unfortunately, many employers could do better. We'll explore how in the following sections.

Job adverts and descriptions

Findings from the Recruitment and Employment Confederation (REC)[1] showed that over half of employers reported that they do not specifically state an interest in diverse candidates in their job adverts.

It is important to review job descriptions and requirements to ensure that each requirement is necessary. For example, if the role doesn't require a full driving licence, take it out. If it doesn't need a degree, don't say it does.

TOP TIP
Watch your language

Kevin Green, CPO at First Bus, suggests that language used in job advertisements and online job sites needs to be engaging, and the message needs to be tailored to the audience.[2] Otherwise, certain marginalized groups may be excluded.

Website

Making sure your website content, including job descriptions, is accessible to everyone can show you are serious about wanting diverse candidates. Consider having an audio option or having fonts and colours accessible for individuals with dyslexia.

Including testimonials from visibly diverse staff on your recruitment page affirms your commitment to EDI. Non-scripted testimonials are more authentic and less likely to be seen as corporate spin. This can really support your employer branding, making you more attractive to diverse applicants.

Website testimonials need to mirror reviews found on job sites like Glassdoor and Indeed, as these sites provide unfiltered comments from current and former employees.

Having testimonials is only an option if there are diverse staff working for you already, and if they have consented to be the poster person(s) for your recruitment campaigns. In the absence of diversity, some organizations will still display diverse imagery on their website, but this may contradict the 'About us' page, if there is a visible lack of diversity in leadership. This might deter diverse applicants because they see an organization where they will not thrive, be welcomed or be successful.

> **KEY POINT**
>
> Placing an advert on your website and expecting diverse talent to apply can be unrealistic if there if nothing else proactively done to attract diverse talent.

Recruitment agencies and boards

If your organization uses a recruitment agency to find talent, there is a risk that they will put forward candidates based on previous placements, knowing they will likely be selected.

One way to attract diverse applicants is to advertise on recruitment boards targeting diverse talent, such as:

- diversejobsmatter.co.uk
- diversitydashboard.co.uk
- diversifying.io
- vercida.com

This can be a very effective way to send a message that you are an inclusive employer wanting to source talent differently.

There are also recruitment diversity platforms relating to a single protected characteristic, as listed below. Google these to find their websites.

WOMEN

- investinginwomen.co.uk
- jobsforwomen.co.uk
- stemwomen.com

DISABILITY

- disabilityjob.co.uk
- evenbreak.com
- neurodiversityjobs.co.uk

BLACK AND MINORITY ETHNIC

- bmejobs.co.uk
- ethnicjobsite.co.uk

LGBTQ+

- lgbtjobs.co.uk
- pink-jobs.com

> **TOP TIP**
> State your intention
>
> Recruitment agencies need clear confirmation that the
> organization wants a diverse pool of candidates, otherwise
> business will be taken elsewhere to bring about change.

Redefining the talent pool

A talent pool is a collection of potential employees that an
organization can draw on to fill open roles. As mentioned in
Chapter 1, organizations able to attract diverse talent give themselves a competitive advantage. Diversity of thought brings
differing perspectives, new ways of thinking and innovation. To
achieve diversity, organizations must redefine their talent pool
and think differently about where they look for talent.

Flexible working

Pre-pandemic, many employers would point to their local geog-
raphy demographics as being one of the main constraints in
attracting diverse talent, even when offering a relocation
package.

However, post-pandemic, the lie 'work is only done in offices'
has been put to bed, mainly by service-centric organizations.
Work, in many instances, can be done from anywhere, if there is

reasonable WIFI connectivity and access to a laptop. While this might not always be true for roles requiring face-to-face engagement, such as roles within manufacturing, healthcare, retail or hospitality, even then, some degree of flexibility can be considered.

Mercer's Global Talent Trends 2024 found that 64 per cent of workers say they are more productive when they work remotely.[3] Additionally, 27 per cent of workers operate in a 50/50 hybrid model, 10 per cent work remotely full-time and an additional 10 per cent work remotely most of the time. 41 per cent of employees said they would only join or stay with an organization if they were able to work remotely at least some of the time, although in 2021, this was higher at 62 per cent.

Notably, 80 per cent of 7,300 respondents in the annual FlexJobs Survey said they would be more loyal to their employers if they had flexible work options, therefore, helping with retention.[4]

Having a flexible approach enables a multitude of talent working differently to be added to the talent pool. This can include return-to-work workers, job sharers, people with disabilities, carers and more.

Steve Collinson, chief HR officer at Zurich UK, underscores this point: 'In 2019, we... introduced our part-time jobs initiative, where all roles are available on a part-time or job-share basis as well as full-time. Overall, applications to the company have been boosted by over 50 per cent... Offering flexibility removes barriers for applicants and enables us to access a whole new pool for talent'.[5]

Gary Cookson, author of *Making Hybrid Working Work*, advocates taking a flexible approach to when, where and how work is done to open the talent pool geographically and from a diversity perspective.[6]

Rethinking sourcing strategies

There are three million people in the UK who are not in work but would like to be, and this includes a whole range of individuals who face barriers, such as the disabled, older workers, carers and parent returners, but also ex-veterans, the homeless, ex-offenders and refugees.

EX-VETERANS

Studies have shown employers are reluctant to hire former military personnel despite veterans scoring in the top 30 per cent for several strengths and capabilities such as social influence, creativity, rational decision making and dealing with ambiguity. Emotional resilience was found to be a particular area of strength.

Jaguar Land Rover, Barclays, Amazon, Deloitte, Network Rail, OpenReach and JP Morgan are part of a Veteran Employers Group (VEG), designed to help more veterans find jobs after leaving the armed forces, launched in 2022 by the government's Office for Veteran Affairs to tackle the barriers faced by ex-veterans.

Ex-veterans can be accessed through platforms like Ex-MilitaryCareers.com.

THE HOMELESS

Crisis, a national homeless charity, states that most homeless people want to work, and that being out of work is both a major cause and consequence of homelessness. Employers can help with this by offering jobs or training programmes.

Morrisons, the retail supermarket, trained 1,000 homeless people in traditional food skills, by offering them apprenticeships or the opportunity to study for basic retailing qualifications, so they could gain loyal and hard-working employees.[7]

EX-OFFENDERS

Seventy-five per cent of employers confirmed they would use the declaration of a criminal record to discriminate against an ex-offender, favouring a candidate with no convictions.

According to the Responsible Business Initiative for Justice (RBIJ),[8] ex-offenders outperformed their co-workers, as they have more to lose and more to prove.

Companies actively hiring ex-offenders include Virgin, Greggs, Greene King and Timpson, using platforms like 'Work with Offenders'.

REAL-WORLD EXAMPLE
Timpson

Timpson is one of the largest employers of ex-offenders in the UK, making up approximately 12 per cent of their workforce. Timpson noted that the vast majority of ex-offenders don't reoffend, are extremely loyal, productive, hardworking and make excellent colleagues, with many being promoted.[9] Timpson believes in offering people work as an alternative to crime, thus helping them break the offending cycle.

REFUGEES

Refugee applicants may hide the fact that they are refugees, due to fear of biased practices.

Refugees have diverse educational and occupational backgrounds, being doctors, engineers or carpenters etc., although legal status can vary from country to country, regarding entitlement to work.

Employees from culturally and linguistically diverse (CALD) backgrounds can deliver in workplaces despite their language skills not being on par with the local workforce.

Research shows employing refugees results in both high productivity and retention rates. There are non-governmental organizations and social enterprises supporting refugee recruitment, like Breaking Barriers. Employers can start small by offering internships, traineeships and short-term or part-time contracting opportunities to one or two refugees.

KEY POINT

By rethinking the definitions of the talent pool, the war for talent can be won.

STOP AND THINK

What categories of difference have you considered when defining talent?

Changing the recruitment process

After attraction, the next stage of the employee's journey is recruitment. In the following, we'll consider how to make the various activities in the recruitment process more conducive for hiring diverse talent.

Diverse recruitment panels

Action needs to be taken to reduce bias inherent in every interview process, whether this is affinity bias, with the recruiting manager wanting to recruit in their own image, or conformity bias, going along with the most powerful voice in the room, which is usually the recruitment manager.

In his book *Competitive People Strategy*, Kevin Green recommends involving a range of people in the assessment activity with different roles and perspectives, as this allows for a diverse set of values to be taken into account, helping to counter any unconscious bias during the process.

According to the responsible business network, Business in the Community (BITC),[10] employers with a policy demanding interview panels to have ethnic minority representation are proven to be more likely to attract and recruit ethnic minority candidates. Having diversity on the panel helps to keep everyone honest, holding each other accountable for their scoring and sends a clear message to the candidates: the organization values difference.

The Recruitment and Employment Confederation (REC) found that 62 per cent reported not using diverse interview panels, which has increased from 56 per cent in 2023 and 53 per cent in 2022.[11]

Organizations lacking diversity at senior levels can train a junior diverse person which can support their development and grant insight into the recruitment process, so they are more confident in applying for roles themselves. A cost-effective alternative could be having diverse externals sit on the panel.

HR practitioners are often part of panels, sometimes as observers or advisers, rather than being equal partners in the process, all depending on how HR is positioned in the organization. Ideally, HR needs to be able to challenge senior leaders and call out any inequity.

STOP AND THINK

- How diverse are your interview panels?
- Do you have guidelines regarding ethnic minority representation?
- Are your panels clear on what they are scoring?
- What involvement does HR have in the interview process?

The process

The best interview panels work by each person on the panel scoring independently on a pre-agreed criteria, and afterwards sharing their scores to discuss and debate, specifically regarding wide discrepancies in scoring. This ensures a robust and fair process.

The recruitment manager should go last, despite usually being the technical expert on the role itself, as they are likely to be the most senior person in the room. Their view could sway other panel members to adjust their scoring due to conformity bias; therefore, going last enables a more robust discussion.

If the interview process involves delivering a presentation or completing an assessment, always consider those who may need additional support, such as neurodivergent candidates. This point may surface in response to candidates being asked what reasonable adjustments would support them. It is a great question, but really, it needs to be asked of all candidates. Surely, you want the candidate to be able to perform to the best of their ability, rather than seeing how you can catch them out.

No two candidates should have the same assessment score across a range of technical hard and personal soft skills, as the goal is appointing the person who is most suited. However, should there be a 'tiebreaker' situation and the organization has a positive action policy, then the person with the protected characteristic can be appointed. (Refer to Chapter 1 for a reminder about positive action.)

TOP TIP
Double check it's a 'tiebreaker'

To warrant a 'tiebreaker' situation, scoring needs to be identical. If there is a point difference between the two candidates, the candidate who has the higher score must be appointed. Failure to appoint on merit would expose the organization to a positive discrimination claim.

KEY POINT

Having a diverse panel and not just a recruitment manager can help mitigate against bias, as can predetermined questions and assessment criteria.

Unconscious bias training

The UK Civil Service decided to scrap unconscious bias training in 2020 after a study found no evidence of its effectiveness on long-term changing behaviour or improving representation.[12] Notably, a tribunal decision in 2021, found a government office guilty of discrimination by unconscious bias. Alexandra Carn, employment law partner at Keystone Law, noted that, '[unconscious bias] training is particularly important for managers and senior managers, not only as they are likely to be key decision-makers, but also to foster an inclusive culture. However, training does have its limitations, and it should be seen as a part of a comprehensive strategy to achieve overall change.'[13]

BITC found that employers that have unconscious bias training have higher ethnic minority recruitment rates.[14] Given that we are all unconsciously biased to varying degrees, there is a need to reduce its impact. Training can assist in self-awareness, so recruitment decisions are more robust. Everyone involved in recruitment needs unconscious bias training, but particularly the recruiting manager, HR and those involved in shortlisting, selection and appointment.

> **TOP TIP**
> Don't just rely on training
>
> Mandated unconscious bias training alone will not lead to any lasting behavioural change, but rather, must be part of a holistic approach.

Short listing

Not every person can be interviewed, so a sifting process needs to take place to arrive at a handful of applicants who can progress to the next stage. This process of narrowing down the applicants to those who will be interviewed can vary from organization to organization.

Some will only consider applicants who have gone to 'red brick' universities, excluding significant numbers of applicants. Others will use AI tools to sift through the applications, using applicant tracking systems with selection based on keywords being cited in the applications.

Cabinet minister, David TC Davies reported he had been rejected by biased AI because he did not have a degree, despite having been the former Welsh Secretary.

Some applicants will be rejected for more questionable reasons. In her book *The Robot-Proof Recruiter*, recruitment specialist Katrina Collier writes about an Australian, Ahmed Imam, who was rejected from over 20 job applications despite being well suited to the roles, so he opted to resubmit his CV for the same jobs under the false name, Adam Smith.[15] He received four calls for an interview the very next day. This example exposes the bias in the shortlisting process, where there is a preference for white-sounding names.

'Adam Smith' is not a lone example. A 2016 study found minorities who practice 'résumé whitening' are more than twice as likely to get a follow-up interview as those who don't.[16] This perhaps explains why several celebrities have changed their names like Chloe Wang, Krishna Pandit Bhanji, Carlos Irwin Estévez, Georgios Panayiotou and Peter Gene Hernandez, although you are more likely to know them as Chloe Bennett, Sir Ben Kingsley, Martin Sheen, George Michael and Bruno Mars.

STOP AND THINK

How does your organization shortlist interview candidates? Do you use AI, and if so, what level of human oversight is there? Is your process at risk from AI bias?

Internal promotions

All the issues and challenges with recruitment and selection apply equally to internal promotions. The questions to address are:

- How are internal opportunities promoted to marginalized groups?
- Are the interview panel members diverse and trained with clear criteria, so that scoring is fair and not skewed?
- How are marginalized individuals encouraged and supported through the process?

STOP AND THINK

Consider the opportunities for internal promotions at your organization. How do you promote them to marginalized groups?

Blind recruitment

Even once you have managed to get a diverse number of candidates to the interview stage, there is a final hurdle to get over. Recruitments can suffer because people can hold a mental image of what the appointable candidate looks like.

This is particularly true for the top job of CEO. According to the CIPD,[17] CEOs are more likely to be called Steve or Stephen than they are to be a woman, based on an analysis of CEOs at the UK's top 100 companies, which found that only six of the CEOs were women. In America's 500 largest companies, there were more CEOs named David than there were female CEOs.[18] Someone's name, like their other visible attributes, does not correlate with their ability or potential. Clearly the recruiting manager had not taken on Shakespeare's advice: 'a rose by any other name would smell as sweet'.

To counter bias in the process, some organizations like the BBC, Virgin Media O2, NHS and Civil Service have embraced 'blind recruitment' as an approach, whereby personally identifiable information is deemed irrelevant to the role and withheld from the recruiting manager and panel. For example, excluding a name reduces gender or racial bias, while 'type of university attended' removes socioeconomic bias.

Coventry City Council used anonymous job applications, resulting in a 117 per cent increase in Black, Asian and minority ethnic candidates, as, with the acknowledgement of unconscious bias and the reassurance that applications will be treated equally, candidates were given the confidence to apply.

The REC found that the majority (75 per cent) of employers do not use blind CV submissions (70 per cent in 2023 and 53 per cent in 2022).[19] Blind recruitment is not an option for internal opportunities, if applicants are known to panel members.

> **KEY POINT**
>
> Blind recruitment is not a magic pill because significant patterns and the use of certain words can lead to gender identification, thus influencing recruiters subconsciously.

Induction

Once a candidate has accepted a job offer, they start in their role and are inducted into the organization. The induction, or 'on boarding' process for an organization can vary from simply, 'here's where you will sit', to a more holistic approach.

Having a proper induction is part of the 'getting to know you' experience beyond initial introduction and first impressions. It involves going beyond what has been gleaned from the website and the interview process, so that a new starter can better understand the organization and decide if it is right for them. It is no surprise, then, that research shows a good induction helps with retention.

The induction process can be an ideal opportunity to stress the importance of EDI to a new starter. It therefore plays a pivotal role in setting the tone for a culturally aware and inclusive workplace.

Inductions do sometimes include mandatory elements of learning, such as safeguarding, data protection and EDI training, which is usually structured as an online training programme with a test at the end to gauge understanding. This type of training is often seen as a tick-box exercise, especially if it is a 'one and done' piece of training. There is value it if it is seen as *part* of the solution rather than the *whole* solution. Carry out refresher training periodically, after the initial induction period has ended (refer to the example of a good induction in the box).

This type of training is also useful as it protects the employer against claims of discrimination and safeguards the employees, by clarifying expectations and behavioural norms. This is aligned with the Equality Act 2010.

TOP TIP

A good induction should consider the needs of all starters and differing ways to engage them to be as inclusive as possible. This could involve using different platforms.

EXAMPLE

An example of a good induction process:

1 A line manager-led induction can introduce the new starter to the role and the team. It can also address issues like health and safety, access to systems and software, as well as support required to process expense claims and recording time worked etc.

2 Thereafter, on a quarterly basis, a two-day induction can be delivered by senior leaders, including HR. These can explain the strategy, wider culture and key HR policies, code of conduct and company values. Here, the expectations can be set for a company culture that treats everyone with dignity and respect.

Training, learning and development

In addition to EDI training being needed for all staff to ensure they are being inclusive towards marginalized groups, there is also a need to ensure that everyone has equal opportunity to be trained and developed.

There are some critical questions to ask:

- Has everyone got the same access to the training they need for their current role and to progress in their career, in the future?
- Is the uptake of training the same across different groups of people?
- Are there any notable differences, between different groups of people in the time it takes to complete the training?
- Are there any notable differences between different groups of people in successfully completing training?
- Has the training led to career progression?
- Is there clarity on the career routes and support available?
- Are there any notable differences between different groups of people with regards to promotions and internal moves?

Fair access to training can vary depending on:

- Geographical location. For example, training that's only available in a capital city may be too costly for those who live outside it.
- Socioeconomic status. Not being able to afford to do the training, if costs are not fully subsidized by the employer.

- Bias in selection. Affinity bias or beauty bias: favouring others over marginalized individuals. Age bias: genuinely believing someone of a certain age is too old to be trained e.g. on digital skills.
- Lacking the right network connections. This may mean someone from a marginalized group is not aware of opportunities or not encouraged by others to put themselves forward.
- Self-deselection: Wherein a marginalized person fears being accused by others of only being selected due to their difference or are led by the belief that nothing beneficial will happen to their career, once the training has been completed.

Successful completion of training can be hindered by barriers and depends on whether:

- Someone is experiencing discrimination from the trainer or fellow trainees, which can derail any learning, taking the focus away from being developed to instead feeling devalued and deflated.
- A person has already been 'left behind' due to systemic inequalities throughout their life, so they are not able to take full advantage of any opportunities presented to them.
- There is a lack of representation and role models, which can impact learning outcomes. This means there is a lack of diversity among trainers/mentors/coaches/peers etc., leaving the trainee with no one to relate to or be inspired by, thus feeling demotivated and isolated.
- There are physical barriers which can hamper the learning potential of those with disabilities, for example, facilities not being accessible to a wheelchair user, or not understanding of the needs of someone with dyslexia.
- There are language barriers which can negatively impact a person's ability to learn, e.g. if English is not the trainee's first language.

• There are social barriers due to cultural reasons or caring responsibilities, such as training taking place in the evenings or weekends.

TOP TIP
Consider training in its broadest sense

Training should not be limited to structured classroom training. Think through all the options:

• On-the-job learning.
• Mentoring.
• Coaching.
• Shadowing.
• Peer-to-peer learning.
• Self-directed learning.
• Networking.
• Action learning sets (a group of people who meet regularly to support each other's learning).

STOP AND THINK

Is there equal opportunity for everyone to access training in your organization?

Remuneration

Remuneration should be straightforward, with everyone being paid a fair wage for work done, irrespective of gender, ethnicity, age, socioeconomic class etc., but that is not the case.

The first attempt to tackle pay parity in the UK was the Equal Pay Act 1970, and sadly, over 50 years on, the issue has still not been resolved. Women are still paid less than men for doing the same or similar work.

Gender pay gaps were introduced in 2017, and while this has not resolved the issue either, it has led to organizations being transparent about the gap: what they intend to do, or are doing to close the gap and actually, reducing the pay gap itself.

While gender pay gap reporting is only a requirement for organizations with over 250 employees, several organizations have opted to report their gender pay gap, even though they are not required to do so. This demonstrates their commitment to transparency and gender equality, by stressing the importance of pay parity to their organization.

According to the Office for National Statistics (ONS), the gender pay gap nationally has been declining, having fallen by approximately a quarter among full-time employees in the last decade, standing at 7.0 per cent in April 2024.[20] Notably, the ONS found the gender pay gap is larger for:

- Employees aged 40 years and over, when compared to those aged under 40 years.
- High earners, compared to lower-paid employees.
- Skilled trades occupations, compared to those in the caring, leisure, and other service occupations.
- Those in England, compared to Wales, Scotland, or Northern Ireland.

PwC 2024 findings suggest it will take another 45 years to achieve gender pay parity, because while the gender gap is reducing each year, the rate of change remains modest.[21]

However, gender pay gap reporting has led to other pay gaps being reported, ahead of being legally required, particularly ethnicity and disability pay gaps. Notably, UNICEF has chosen to embrace pay gap reporting fully and is reporting on six pay gaps: ethnicity, disability, sexual orientation, intersectionality for gender and ethnicity, LGBTQIA+ using colleagues' declared gender rather than that assigned at birth.[22]

STOP AND THINK

What pay gaps are currently reported on in your organization? Do some research to find out if necessary. Which pay gap would it be beneficial to understand further?

WHAT WOULD YOU DO?
Number 6

Ayotunde, a young female of Nigerian heritage, has come to you to complain that John, an older white male, has been appointed into a role without any process purely based on his friendship and shared interests with Kevin, the recruiting manager. Kevin is also white, male and of a similar age. You raise this with Kevin, who assures you John was perfect for the demanding role.

- What are the concerns with this approach?
- What would you advise Kevin?

CHAPTER SUMMARY

- Attracting diverse talent should not be left to a one-size-fits-all advertisement. Careful consideration must be given to the wording and placement.
- Talent needs to be considered more broadly to include more diverse groups of people.
- Diverse panels with clear assessment criteria and adjustments to the process will enable diverse talent to progress to appointment, supported by a good induction.
- There are numerous barriers faced by diverse talent in accessing training, learning and development, which need to be considered.

- Pay gaps are useful for surfacing inequity across different protected characteristics.

REVIEW QUESTIONS

1 Why is it important to have diversity in leadership to attract diverse talent?

2 Name three ways organizations can rethink their sourcing strategies.

3 When would positive action be used in an interview situation?

4 What is blind recruitment?

Endnotes

1 https://www.hrmagazine.co.uk/content/news/employers-losing-focus-on-inclusive-hiring (archived at https://perma.cc/98VK-DL4H)

2 Green, K (2019) *Competitive People Strategy: How to attract, develop and retain the staff you need for business success*, Kogan Page

3 https://www.mercer.com/assets/global/en/shared-assets/local/attachments/pdf-2024-global-talent-trends-report-en.pdf (archived at https://perma.cc/74RJ-5V2E)

4 https://www.flexjobs.com/blog/post/survey-flexible-work-job-choices (archived at https://perma.cc/3SER-J4VM)

5 https://www.hrmagazine.co.uk/content/news/uk-workers-given-day-one-flexible-working-rights (archived at https://perma.cc/46TH-FL8J)

6 Cookson, G, *Making Hybrid Working Work*, Kogan Page

7 https://hrzone.com/morrisons-to-employ-and-train-1000-homeless (archived at https://perma.cc/DE2P-NJ66)

8 https://www.hrmagazine.co.uk/content/features/employers-mustnt-be-afraid-to-recruit-ex-offenders (archived at https://perma.cc/GR73-GJ27)

9 https://www.timpson-group.co.uk/timpson-foundation/ex-offenders (archived at https://perma.cc/ZV99-489B)

10   https://www.hrmagazine.co.uk/content/news/employers-that-have-unconscious-bias-training-have-higher-ethnic-minority-recruitment-rates-says-bitc-report (archived at https://perma.cc/C9LW-9DDS)

11   https://www.hrmagazine.co.uk/content/news/employers-losing-focus-on-inclusive-hiring (archived at https://perma.cc/98VK-DL4H)

12   https://www.gov.uk/government/publications/unconscious-bias-and-diversity-training-what-the-evidence-says (archived at https://perma.cc/WD6Q-6E84)

13   https://www.hrmagazine.co.uk/content/news/government-office-found-guilty-of-discrimination-by-unconscious-bias (archived at https://perma.cc/8E2R-NR7M)

14   https://www.hrmagazine.co.uk/content/news/employers-that-have-unconscious-bias-training-have-higher-ethnic-minority-recruitment-rates-says-bitc-report (archived at https://perma.cc/C9LW-9DDS)

15   Collier, K (2022) *The Robot-Proof Recruiter: A survival guide for recruitment and sourcing professionals*, Kogan Page

16   https://journals.sagepub.com/doi/abs/10.1177/0001839216639577?journalCode=asqa (archived at https://perma.cc/ZR4Y-6A7P)

17   https://www.independent.co.uk/life-style/ceo-women-business-sexism-ftse-100-a9073391.html (archived at https://perma.cc/MAY8-6QDA)

18   https://www.onemodel.co/blog/davids (archived at https://perma.cc/7H8Z-JRAH)

19   https://www.hrmagazine.co.uk/content/news/employers-losing-focus-on-inclusive-hiring (archived at https://perma.cc/98VK-DL4H)

20   https://www.ons.gov.uk/employmentandlabourmarket/peopleinwork/earningsandworkinghours/bulletins/genderpaygapintheuk/2024 (archived at https://perma.cc/8PHB-WEAH)

21   https://www.pwc.co.uk/human-resource-services/assets/pdfs/year-7-gender-pay-gap-report-2023-2024.pdf (archived at https://perma.cc/JPT3-CAKN)

22   https://www.peoplemanagement.co.uk/article/1894815/unicef-uks-martyn-dicker-were-reporting-six-pay-gaps-counting---its-blunt-tool-its-tool (archived at https://perma.cc/TC52-5CJY)

CHAPTER SEVEN

How discrimination shows up

Introduction

Richard Branson's assertion, 'If you take care of your employees, they will take care of the clients', underscores the importance of a safe and inclusive workplace being essential for employees to do their best work. This sets the tone nicely for this chapter.

The Young Foundation's 2024 survey found that 72 per cent of professionals say they have experienced discriminatory or exclusionary workplace behaviour, and 73 per cent have experienced barriers to progression in their career.[1]

Research by the Young Women's Trust found that young women face increasing challenges, with 53 per cent reporting discrimination at work in 2024, an increase from 42 per cent in 2022.[2] Age-based discrimination also persists, affecting both younger and older workers, according to Mercer's Global Talent Trends.[3]

Despite these issues, the Resolution Foundation found that less than 1 per cent of reported discrimination cases reach tribunals.[4] This may be due to gaslighting, where individuals are made to question their perceptions, or fear of retaliation, leading to underreporting.

Understanding the nuances of discrimination, bullying, harassment and victimization is important for effectively addressing these challenges and promoting a supportive work environment to focus EDI efforts. We consider all of these issues in this chapter, as well as cases related to each one. As you read this chapter, consider whether there is a particular marginalized group that is alienated and disproportionately subject to performance management, disciplinary actions, grievances or high staff turnover within your own organization.

LEARNING OBJECTIVES

By the end of this chapter, you will be able to:

• Understand the types of discrimination.

• Appreciate the difference between bullying and harassment.

• Explore the varied routes to resolution.

• Assess whether dismissals are fair and any EDI implications.

Types of discrimination

Aggrieved parties often allege discrimination, bullying, harassment and victimization, using the terms interchangeably over the way they feel unfairly treated or targeted, because they have been performance managed or disciplined or exited by the employer. It is possible one of those things has happened, but it is unlikely they all have occurred.

Direct discrimination

Direct discrimination tends to be very overt and relates to when a person receives less favourable treatment due to a protected characteristic. An example might be if a job description asks for recent graduates or those with no more than two years' experience, thereby discouraging older applicants from applying.

REAL-WORLD EXAMPLE
London and Quadrant Housing Trust[5]

Two employees (current and former) won a direct discrimination claim against London and Quadrant Housing Trust based on their race and were awarded £95,000. They were overlooked for promotions. The successful applicants were white, and were therefore appointed, based on who would fit in. The hiring manager opted not to record all the information provided during the interviews, and the HR recruitment adviser deferred to the hiring manager.

Discrimination by association

Discrimination by association is a type of direct discrimination against someone due to their connection with a person or group who has a protected characteristic. From the point it becomes known that Person A is friends with someone who is Black, Person A is subsequently treated unfavourably, even though Person A does not share that racial characteristic. Discrimination by association does not apply to the protected characteristic of marriage and civil partnership.

Discrimination by perception

Discriminating against someone because of the misconception that they have a certain protected characteristic, is also a type of direct discrimination. For example, discriminating against someone with a beard and a turban because you think they are a Muslim, but they are Sikh, would still be discrimination. Discrimination by perception does not apply to the protected characteristic of marriage and civil partnership.

Indirect discrimination

Indirect discrimination is far more subtle than direct discrimination. It relates to a person being treated less favourably because of a protected characteristic. For example, an advert stipulating a height requirement of over 172 centimetres for someone to stack shelves in a supermarket seems appropriate, given the duties involved. A shorter person would struggle to safely reach higher shelves... right? Wrong!

When you consider the average height of a man is around 172 centimetres, this advert is discriminating against women, who tend to be shorter, and favouring men, without explicitly stating it.

The requirements of the role do not provide a justifiable excuse for being discriminatory. A shorter person, irrespective of gender, could use steps to reach the higher shelves, so it is not an insurmountable challenge.

REAL-WORLD EXAMPLE
London Underground Limited versus Edwards[6]

Edwards, a single mother, struggled to balance work and childcare after London Underground introduced a new shift system.

The Employment Appeal Tribunal found that the shift system constituted indirect sex discrimination, as it disproportionately affected women with childcare responsibilities when compared to men, considering women are more likely to bear primary childcare responsibilities.

Victimization

In the context of the Equality Act 2010, victimization differs from our usual understanding of a victim as someone who suffers harassment or bullying.

Victimization occurs when someone is treated less favourably because of being involved with a discrimination or harassment complaint, which could be their own complaint or as a witness to someone else's complaint.

For example, Person A files a complaint about a protected characteristic and later receives a low performance rating despite good yearly performance. Or alternatively, Person X files a complaint regarding a protected characteristic and lists Person Y as a witness. Following this, Person Y is not considered for a promotion, despite meeting all the requirements and being a strong internal candidate.

Victimization is a punitive action taken in response to someone raising a complaint, related to a protected characteristic. This punitive action could result in the complainant being seen as a troublemaker, excluded and denied opportunities. If someone maliciously provides false evidence or makes a false allegation of discrimination or harassment, then a claim of victimization would not be upheld.

REAL-WORLD EXAMPLE
Ms L Callaghan versus Lidl Great Britain[7]

Callaghan, a former Lidl employee, raised a complaint against the regional head, Mr Carter, alleging she was made to feel uncomfortable when he had held her face with both hands, pressured her to go swimming and didn't allow her to wear her coat to discretely access sanitary products, among other allegations.

An internal investigation did not support Callaghan's complaints, but another allegation was subsequently raised that Carter had been ignoring her since the start of the investigation.

Due to the way Lidl managed her complaints about Carter's behaviour, Callaghan was awarded over £22,000 as compensation for her claims of sex discrimination and victimization.

KEY POINT

A person can be a victim without necessarily having been victimized.

Microaggressions

Microaggressions are typically minor in the bigger scheme of behaviours and can often go unnoticed, particularly if organizations are less sensitized to this kind of behaviour. However, someone from a minority background, who is on the receiving end of microaggressions, is more likely to note these behaviours. Individually, they may not seem harmful, but over time, their cumulative effect can be damaging. Effectively, microaggressions can be the equivalent of death by a '1,000 cuts'. Each individual cut may lead to a single drop of blood, but a '1,000 cuts' results in much more blood being shed.

Microaggressions can be something said verbally or in writing, and can be an action or inaction, targeting marginalized individuals, but it can be hard to prove that these are related to a protected characteristic.

To address microaggressions, global law firm Hogan Lovells launched a platform in 2024 for lawyers to anonymously report microaggressions or incidents related to gender, race, sexual orientation and disability.[8] This was done to ensure every voice is heard, allowing them to review and act on trends.

REAL-WORLD EXAMPLE
Viveak Taneja versus Bathroom Trading Company Ltd[9]

Taneja, a British Indian salesperson, was repeatedly called 'V', instead of his full name, by his employer, despite stating his desire to be called by his actual name. The tribunal concluded that this created a hostile work environment and was racial harassment, awarding Mr Taneja over £9,000 in compensation.

TOP TIP
Be alert to microaggressions

Microaggressions can be subtle. An example could be someone frowning or rolling their eyes every time a specific person speaks.

Another could be repeatedly asking someone where they are really from.

Harassment

The terms 'harassment' and 'bullying' are often used interchangeably. While there are certain similarities, they are very distinct, primarily because the former relates to protected characteristics and the latter does not.

To be clear, whether it is harassment or bullying, nobody comes to work to have their dignity taken away from them, and no employer can pay enough to think they have the right to violate someone else.

Harassment and bullying occur because some employers believe they can act with impunity, which is why the Equality Act 2010 is crucial in addressing the former at least.

There are three types of harassment defined by the Equality Act 2010.

1 Harassment related to certain 'protected characteristics'.
2 Sexual harassment.
3 Less favourable treatment as a result of harassment.

Harassment related to certain 'protected characteristics'

The protected characteristics we are talking about in this case are age, disability, gender reassignment, race, religion or belief, sex and sexual orientation.

To be classified as harassment, the concerns must be related to unwanted behaviour, which has either violated the person's dignity, or created an intimidating, hostile, degrading, humiliating or offensive environment for the person, irrespective if it was intended or not, and regardless of whether it was intended to have this effect.

The decision on whether something is harassment or not depends on (a) the circumstances of the situation, (b) how the person receiving the unwanted behaviour views it and (c) if the person receiving the unwanted behaviour is 'reasonable' to view it as harassment.

The intent of the harasser is secondary to how the victim perceives the harassment. The perpetrator may argue, 'I did not intend it to be interpreted that way.' However, if the recipient perceives the actions or comments as offensive and demeaning, it may be classified as harassment.

Harassment does not have to be a series of incidents. It may occur frequently or be an isolated incident. For example saying 'good morning love' to a colleague every day at work for the last five years might have been accepted by the recipient as banter, but should that person decide otherwise and say, 'Well actually I am not your love, so don't refer to me in such a way again', it is at this point it becomes harassment, should it continue.

Unwanted behaviour can include: a serious one-off incident, repeated behaviour, spoken or written words, imagery, graffiti, gestures, mimicry, jokes, pranks and physical behaviour, affecting the person and leaving them feeling disrespected, frightened, humiliated, insulted, intimidated or threatened.

Perpetrators will often gaslight their victims to excuse and justify their behaviour, for example, telling the victim they are being overly sensitive.

Gaslighting: This is a form of abuse involving manipulating a person so that they start to doubt their own reality or experience.

> **REAL-WORLD EXAMPLE**
> **Mr Alexander Martin Cubbin versus Age UK 2024**[10]
>
> Mr Cubbin's claim that Age UK subjected him to harassment, related to his age was upheld by the Employment Tribunal and he was awarded £4,000 as compensation for injury to feelings. This example highlights that, even in a charity like Age UK, expected to be more aware of age-related harassment, they can still fall foul of the Equality Act 2010.

Sexual harassment

Sexual harassment also relates to unwanted behaviour of a sexual nature, applicable to employees and workers, contractors and self-employed people hired to personally do the work, and job applicants.

The concerns have to be related to unwanted behaviour, which has either violated the person's dignity, or created an intimidating, hostile, degrading, humiliating or offensive environment for the person, irrespective of whether it was intended or not and regardless of whether it was intended to have this effect.

As covered in Chapter 1, the Worker Protection Act 2023 has a duty for employers to prove they have taken all reasonable steps to prevent sexual harassment by employees, 'agents' and third parties in the workplace.

Employers have vicarious liability, meaning the employer can be responsible for employees' discriminatory actions linked to work. Vicarious liability extends beyond the workplace to events like after-hours gatherings and social media platforms.

Employers also have a duty of care to safeguard their employees, which, if they fail to do, could lead to an employee feeling they have no choice but to resign and make a claim for constructive dismissal, as well as sexual harassment.

Sexual harassment can occur between people of any gender or sexual orientation. In the workplace, sexual harassment can involve colleagues, customers, clients, suppliers, as well as members of the public in relation to work.

Sexual harassment can be a one-off incident, or an ongoing pattern of behaviour, and can be in person, but not necessarily, as it includes virtual interactions, such as online meetings, email communications, social media or messaging tools.

Examples can include the following: Making sexual remarks about someone's body, clothing or appearance; asking questions about someone's sex life; telling sexually offensive jokes; making sexual comments or jokes about someone's sexual orientation or gender reassignment; displaying or sharing pornographic or sexual images, or other sexual content; touching someone against their will, for example hugging them, sexual assault or rape.

REAL-WORLD EXAMPLE
McDonalds[11]

Seven hundred current and former employees, aged 19 or younger, have filed claims of sexual harassment, across 450 restaurants. There are also allegations of discrimination, homophobia, racism and ableism.

Allegations of sexual harassment were made, involving managers engaging in inappropriate touching and instances of harassment by customers. However, it was reported that no action was taken when these incidents were brought to attention.

The Chief Executive of McDonalds confirmed they had received 75 allegations of sexual harassment, upholding 47 claims and leading to 29 people being dismissed.

Note that there is a significant disparity between the number of claims by 700 current and former staff, compared to the relatively low number of 75 allegations considered by McDonalds.

Following an initial investigation in July 2023, the Equality and Human Rights Commission has since written to all branches in Britain advising them to comply with their legal duties or risk enforcement action, where an unlimited fine could be issued.[12]

> **TOP TIP**
> Beware of banter and gaslighting
>
> Sexual remarks and 'jokes' are often excused as banter, but this is not a defence. The victim may also be gaslighted for being overly sensitive.

Less favourable treatment as a result of harassment

This third category applies to someone who is treated less favourably because of how they responded to previous harassment, irrespective of whether they rejected or submitted to the harassment. For example, a manager makes sexual advances towards a direct report, and regardless of whether the direct report accepts or rejects the sexual advances, the manager now starts to treat the direct report less favourably.

The previous harassment must be related to either (a) sexual harassment, (b) harassment related to sex or (c) harassment related to gender reassignment but not marriage and civil partnership, nor pregnancy and maternity.

Hate crimes

In England, Scotland and Wales, some types of harassment could be a hate crime, constituting a criminal offence, if it relates to disability, race, religion, sexual orientation or being transgender. Age is a considered factor in Scotland as well.

Hate crimes tend to be overt and particularly harmful, such as physical violence, sexual assault, verbal abuse, threats of violence, online abuse, damage to someone's property and inciting or stirring up hatred.

Victims of suspected hate crimes can report to the police. If there is an ongoing risk, the employer may contact the police but must inform and support the victim. The victim can separately raise a complaint through the grievance process, separate from any police criminal investigation.

> **KEY POINT**
>
> While an employee relations investigation is based on the balance of probabilities, the burden of proof for a criminal investigation is much higher. A police investigation without charges does not guarantee the same outcome in an employee relations investigation.

> **PROTECTION FROM HARASSMENT ACT 1997**
>
> There is one additional type of harassment distinct from the three listed under the Equality Act 2010.
>
> An individual is protected from any behaviour causing alarm or distress, but does not necessarily have to be connected to a protected characteristic. For example, stalking could constitute a criminal act.

Bullying

Research conducted by the legal services business, Wright Hassall, found the following:[13]

- 50 per cent of people have either been bullied at work or witnessed it.
- 57 per cent think shouting at work doesn't count as bullying.
- 35 per cent of people didn't think jokes about a person could be considered bullying.
- 32 per cent of people didn't believe exclusion from group meetings to be bullying behaviour.
- 63 per cent of people felt abrupt emails wouldn't be classed as bullying.

- 12 per cent didn't think intimidation was bullying.
- 21 per cent didn't think spreading rumours about a person crossed the threshold into bullying.
- 6 per cent didn't believe any of the previously mentioned behaviours would be considered bullying.

This research reflects a broad problem: bullying is shrouded in ambiguity. As Alan Sharland, Director of CAOS Conflict Management notes, 'As a consequence of the ambiguity around what constitutes bullying, almost all investigations into allegations are inconclusive and therefore immensely frustrating for all affected – both the person who feels "bullied" and the person accused of being "the bully".'[14]

There is no legal definition of bullying. The Advisory, Conciliation and Arbitration Service (ACAS),[15] describes bullying as unwanted behaviour from a person or group that is either 1) offensive, intimidating, malicious or insulting or 2) an abuse or misuse of power that undermines, humiliates or causes physical or emotional harm to someone.

Bullying can be a regular pattern of behaviour or a one-off incident; it can happen face-to-face or on social media, in emails or calls. It can happen at work or in other work-related situations, and not always be obvious or noticed by others.

It is understandable why bullying is frequently mistaken for harassment, and vice versa, as several descriptors are identical, as emphasized in italics below.

Harassment, like bullying, also relates to *unwanted behaviour* creating an *intimidating*, hostile, degrading, *humiliating* or *offensive* environment.

ACAS clarifies that unless bullying amounts to conduct defined as harassment in the Equality Act 2010, it is not possible to make a complaint to an employment tribunal about it.

> **TOP TIP**
> Look beyond the protected characteristics
>
> Bullying can involve any differences, beyond the nine protected characteristics, including body shape, facial features, regional accents, hair style and social class.

Power imbalance

Dutch social psychologist Geert Hofstede suggested power distance – the extent to which people accept unequal power distribution – is one of six cultural dimensions, in which hierarchical organizations typically have their authority respected, not questioned or challenged by those lower in the hierarchy, due to an unequal distribution of power.[16] This can allow managers to exert significant influence over their direct reports, who are more likely to be compliant. Those in insecure work, such as fixed-term contracts, casual contracts, freelancers or those in their early careers are at greater risk of power imbalance.

Bullying persists due to victims fearing retaliation or ostracism should they speak up, thus discouraging victims and bystanders from reporting it. It is also enabled by weak leaders who ignore inappropriate behaviours.

> **KEY POINT**
>
> Since diversity is often found lower in the hierarchy, abuse will disproportionately be targeted at minority groups.

Legal remedies to bullying

The Protection from Harassment Act 1997 clarified that employers can be held 'vicariously liable' for the misconduct of their employees, but in this instance the bullying must be deemed 'oppressive and unacceptable' and 'calculated in an objective sense to cause alarm or distress', also meeting the threshold for criminal liability.

If the bullying is physical and threatening, there may be options to pursue a criminal charge. However, if the bullying is less severe, the only legal remedy available would be to raise a complaint under the duty of the employer towards the employee regarding health and wellbeing, or for the employee to resign and claim constructive dismissal, due to the breach of the implied term of trust and confidence.

David Liddle notes in his extensive career of mediating cases of bullying, he has rarely come across a true example of 'bullying', but has rather found instances of 'miscommunication, misperceptions and an alarming lack of ability among managers to have meaningful, compassionate and collaborative conversations with their teams'.[17]

TOP TIP
Have clear policies and a code of conduct

Having clear policies on bullying, discrimination, values and a code of conduct can help to clarify expectations while actions taken in response to bullying and discrimination set the tone for the whole organization.

Resolution

When an employee raises a grievance, it can feel like they are against the whole organization, with HR siding with management. They have access to employment lawyers, while the aggrieved person may only have union representation, assuming they were a member before the incident.

Often, issues lack evidence and boil down to uncorroborated 'he said, she said' statements. Even when there is documentation or witnesses, interpretations vary, or witnesses may be unwilling to participate. This does not mean nothing has happened, rather, it cannot be proven.

People rarely point-blank admit to the thing they are accused of. At best, they might tell you they have been misunderstood and misrepresented, but most will deny the allegations completely.

Trust and relationships often break down, which is almost inevitable. Accusations of harassment or bullying are serious and unpleasant. Usually, people do not intend to be harmful; it's often seen as just work. However, for the victim, it feels personal as work impacts their time, livelihood, security and family.

Mediation

Restorative justice in EDI focuses on repairing harm and restoring relationships through accountability and meaningful dialogue. Mediation is the best way to resolve most workplace disputes, aiming for an agreement on future cooperation. The discussion should acknowledge past events without assigning blame and focus on future changes. This mediation conversation needs to be facilitated by a trained mediator and not left to individuals to manage alone without support.

Mediation should never be used to downplay or ignore discrimination. We are all fallible and mistakes will happen. Mediation could be considered as part of the resolution process, eliminating the need to resort to a grievance. This helps to avoid breaking the working relationship, because even if a grievance is successfully upheld, the working relationship is forever damaged, and issues may well reoccur.

KEY POINT

Disputes are rarely black and white. Each party normally has some responsibility for their actions and decisions.

Non-disclosure agreements

When an employee is considering pursuing a tribunal claim, normally it is because they have exhausted routes like mediation or the internal grievance procedures and are still aggrieved, because their claim has not been upheld or is only partially upheld.

A tribunal claim is likely to take up the claimant's time and energy, rather than them actively securing new employment, and can take anything between six months for simple cases and up to two years for more complex cases. This can be very costly, while keeping the aggrieved party focused on what has happened in the past, rather than thinking about their best interests for the future.

Even if a person wins at a tribunal, the usual remedy is financial compensation, rather than reinstatement into the role. Additionally, there is a possibility that future employers may view them as litigious, which could affect their professional reputation.

One of the routes to resolution is having a 'without prejudice' conversation to arrive at a settlement, using a non-disclosure agreement (NDA). This can be more helpful to both the employee and employer, especially where the relationship has completely broken down, having impacted the employee, both physically and mentally, and the employer delivering the products and services.

Therefore, signing an NDA might seem like a win-win, but if the claim was related to discrimination and harassment, then the victim has been silenced and removed, while the perpetrator has continued to stay in post with no consequences for their alleged behaviour. This sends a message to the wider organization that inappropriate behaviour is okay, further enabling discrimination and harassment, while also creating a culture of silence.

Can't Buy My Silence found that NDAs disproportionately affected women and low-income workers.[18] NDAs should support the claimant, not protect the perpetrator. It is important to surface any EDI concerns so that they are called out, addressed and not 'swept under the carpet'.

KEY POINT

In January 2025, the UK government confirmed it would implement the Higher Education (Freedom of Speech) Act 2023, which bans the use of NDAs to silence victims of bullying, harassment or sexual misconduct on campus, with campaigners wanting to see this extended to all workplaces.[19]

Tribunal claims and compensation

If an allegation of discrimination is made and not resolved internally through complaints and grievances processes, then the aggrieved party can submit a claim to the tribunals, where if successful, the claimant will be awarded compensation.

For some claimants, no amount of money will suffice, as they are fighting for the principles they believe have been violated and want their day in court.

The maximum and average amount awarded can vary depending on the specifics of each claim, which includes the type and severity of discrimination, the impact on the individual, and the circumstances surrounding the incident. Table 7.1 shows awards per discrimination type between April 2023 and March 2024 in the UK.[20]

TABLE 7.1   Maximum and average awards per discrimination type in the UK

Discrimination type	Maximum award	Average award
Sex	£995,128	£53,403
Disability	£964,465	£44,483
Race	£431,768	£29,532
Age	£261,949	£102,891
Sexual orientation	£47,297	£27,070
Religion and belief	£20,000	£10,750

There were some notable cases in 2024:

- Rachael Wright-Turner was awarded nearly £4.6 million after an employment tribunal found she had been subjected to disability discrimination and harassment by the London Borough of Hammersmith and Fulham.[21]
- Nicola Hinds received over £350,000 after an employment tribunal found her employer, Mitie, had discriminated against her due to her pregnancy, dismissing her concerns as hormonal behaviour.[22]
- Glenn Cowie, a 58-year-old executive was awarded over £3 million in damages for age discrimination, victimization and unfair dismissal, after being called an 'old fossil' by his boss.[23]
- Mrs J Ware was awarded over £173,000 after an employment tribunal found she had been unfairly dismissed and directly discriminated against because of her age after being told, 'We won't be here forever'.[24]

The point being made is that, allowing discrimination to occur can be a costly affair for the employer. In addition to the costs of compensation, considerable costs may be incurred, such as legal fees in defending these claims, as well as management time. Notably most claims do not reach tribunal, but are settled beforehand, so these costs have not been reflected above.

Dismissals

A person can leave an organization voluntarily or involuntarily.

Voluntary turnover

When someone leaves voluntarily, further inquiry may be needed, even if no other reasons were mentioned in their exit interview (assuming these are done):

· Was this person being paid less than their market worth?
· Was this person not able to secure a promotion internally?
· Has this person been unable to develop their career?
· Were the policies supportive of those with caring responsibilities or health issues?
· Did they want a career break? Could a sabbatical have been considered?

Leadership consulting firm DDI's Frontline Leader Project found that 57 per cent of employees have left a job due to their manager, with an additional 32 per cent seriously considering leaving for the same reason.[25] All these are potentially EDI issues.

Exit interviews may have limited value, because staff often avoid negative comments to secure a good reference. Additionally, employees might be cautious about sharing information, as they may not trust what will be done with it.

> **TOP TIP**
> Enhance your exit interviews
>
> Consider having an external provider conduct your exit interviews, three to six months after the employee's departure. By then, they are likely to be in a role elsewhere and may feel more able to provide candid responses, potentially highlighting EDI concerns.

Involuntary turnover

Involuntary turnover is initiated by the employer and can be classified as fair or unfair dismissals, according to employment law.

There are four main grounds for fair dismissals, which are as follows:

1 Capability or performance: The employee lacks the capability to do their job properly, such as not having the right skills or ill health.
2 Conduct: The employee engages in serious or gross misconduct, e.g. theft or harassment.
3 Redundancy: A job role is not required, due to changes in the business environment, such as downsizing or restructuring.
4 Legality: Staying employed would break the law, e.g. a driver losing their licence, essential for the role.

Finally, 'some other substantial reason' (SOSR) would potentially address any other scenarios. All other dismissals would be regarded as unfair, if there are underlying discriminatory concerns, related to the protected characteristics. For example, Pregnant Then Screwed found that potentially 74,000 women a year are fired or made redundant while pregnant or on maternity leave.

REAL-WORLD EXAMPLE
Mr W Norman versus Lidl Great Britain Ltd[26]

Wayne Norman was made redundant from Lidl during a restructuring, partly because he lacked a degree or qualification used as the selection criterion. Norman claimed this was indirect age discrimination, as aged 60 years old, he would not have a qualification.

The tribunal found that Norman was treated unfairly in the criteria used and his dismissal was also unfair, as he couldn't contest his redundancy selection scoring.

KEY POINT

In dismissal cases that are due to capability or redundancy, it is crucial to ensure that there has been no discrimination against the employee. Otherwise, this may be deemed an unfair dismissal by a tribunal.

WHAT WOULD YOU DO?
Number 7

Saoirse, finds herself consistently excluded from key meetings, her ideas are frequently dismissed, and she has received vague but increasingly negative feedback from her manager. When Saoirse raises concerns informally, she is told to 'toughen up' and that she might be 'overthinking it'. Fearing she might be labelled as a troublemaker, she resigns, citing vague reasons.

- What are the red flags?
- What action can you take?

CHAPTER SUMMARY

- Types of discrimination include direct, indirect, association and perception-based.
- Harassment is covered by the Equality Act 2010 and is distinct from bullying, which is not associated with the protected characteristics.
- Resolution routes can include mediation, NDAs or tribunal claims, but any EDI issues need to be addressed.
- Employees can exit an organization voluntarily or involuntarily, but this needs to be a fair dismissal, recognizing any discriminatory behaviour.

REVIEW QUESTIONS

1 How is indirect discrimination different from direct discrimination?
2 What are the legal remedies for bullying?
3 What are the risks linked to using NDAs?
4 What makes a dismissal unfair?

Endnotes

1 https://www.youngfoundation.org/insights/news/nearly-three-in-four-professionals-say-they-experience-discriminatory-or-exclusionary-workplace-behaviour (archived at https://perma.cc/74A6-6HFZ)

2 https://www.youngwomenstrust.org/our-research/a-world-not-designed-for-us-annual-survey-2024 (archived at https://perma.cc/UX4V-BAR6)

3 https://www.mercer.com/assets/global/en/shared-assets/local/attachments/pdf-2024-global-talent-trends-report-en.pdf (archived at https://perma.cc/74RJ-5V2E)

4 https://www.hrmagazine.co.uk/content/news/less-than-1-of-discrimination-reports-reach-tribunal (archived at https://perma.cc/Y5JN-H6RK)

5 https://www.equalityhumanrights.com/housing-association-employees-win-race-discrimination-case (archived at https://perma.cc/PV96-X9JP)

6 https://www.equalrightstrust.org/ertdocumentbank/Microsoft%20Word%20-%20London%20Underground.pdf (archived at https://perma.cc/SJ27-S4K2)

7 https://www.personneltoday.com/hr/lidl-sex-discrimination-callaghan-tribunal (archived at https://perma.cc/SJY5-UX7J)

8 https://www.lawgazette.co.uk/news/city-firm-wants-staff-to-call-out-microaggressions/5120172.article (archived at https://perma.cc/2ARV-4FNK)

9 https://www.hrmagazine.co.uk/content/news/repeatedly-misnaming-employee-is-race-harassment-tribunal-rules (archived at https://perma.cc/9F3M-BAZ9)

10 https://www.civilsociety.co.uk/news/age-uk-ordered-to-pay-4-000-after-losing-age-related-harassment-case.html (archived at https://perma.cc/7LZP-L3UT)

11 https://www.peoplemanagement.co.uk/article/1901691/mcdonalds-sexual-harassment-allegations-hr-learn? (archived at https://perma.cc/65VH-GG9E)

12 https://www.equalityhumanrights.com/media-centre/news/our-letter-mcdonalds-franchises (archived at https://perma.cc/M4YR-X4ZK)

13 https://www.wrighthassall.co.uk/knowledge-base/over-half-of-uk-employees-think-shouting-at-work-isn-t-bullying (archived at https://perma.cc/3FHP-ZRBT)

14 https://hrzone.com/bullying-in-the-workplace-the-illusion-of-bullying-versus-the-reality-of-harassment (archived at https://perma.cc/KV4D-T3FY)

15 https://www.acas.org.uk/bullying-at-work (archived at https://perma.cc/LP37-XL78)

16 https://www.verywellmind.com/hofstedes-cultural-dimensions-8583990? (archived at https://perma.cc/B4D8-QLWQ)

17 https://hrzone.com/bullying-isnt-always-a-binary-issue-how-to-make-sure-your-hr-processes-dont-make-it-one/ (archived at https://perma.cc/S6G2-XZBD)

18 https://www.personneltoday.com/hr/louise-haigh-two-tier-nda
    (archived at https://perma.cc/PAG5-7AST)
19 https://www.gov.uk/government/news/government-reaffirms-
    commitment-to-free-speech-in-universities (archived at
    https://perma.cc/99SE-AKCU)
20 https://worknest.com/blog/employment-tribunals-figures-reveal-
    marked-increase-cases-compensatory-awards (archived at
    https://perma.cc/PUZ4-L9M3)
21 https://www.personneltoday.com/hr/ptsd-tribunal-grenfell-disability-
    discrimination-wright-turner-hammersmith-fulham (archived at
    https://perma.cc/E787-7PM9)
22 https://www.hrmagazine.co.uk/content/news/calling-pregnant-
    employee-emotional-was-discrimination-tribunal-rules (archived at
    https://perma.cc/M2LV-H7MJ)
23 https://www.personneltoday.com/hr/executive-called-old-fossil-
    awarded-3-2m-in-ageism-case (archived at https://perma.cc/QS69-
    8E6Q)
24 https://www.personneltoday.com/hr/age-discrimination-forever-ware-
    ealing-horsenden-primary-school (archived at https://perma.cc/
    7AWH-P55A)
25 https://www.hrdive.com/news/employees-really-do-leave-bad-bosses-
    research-shows/568774 (archived at https://perma.cc/W6TF-V3N9)
26 https://www.personneltoday.com/hr/degree-age-discrimination-
    redundancy-selection-ageism-norman-v-lidl (archived at
    https://perma.cc/537A-8Y4Z)

CHAPTER EIGHT

Making the case for EDI

Introduction

The world of work is directly affected by global events, which materialize one after the other, and sometimes simultaneously. We are all living through perpetual change, so it is no surprise that one of the Collins Dictionary's words of the year in 2022 was 'permacrisis', because we are in a permanent state of crisis, with the rate of change and instability approaching faster than ever.

All this has an impact on EDI within organizations. Social and political shifts can move EDI up and down agendas, and the role of the EDI practitioner can become much harder overnight.

This chapter considers how to navigate pushback against EDI initiatives and why that pushback can happen. We look at the importance of being clear about what initiatives aim to achieve and why they are important, and being able to answer how EDI initiatives will help organizations to achieve their short and long-term goals. We consider how to get buy-in from senior leaders and build a business case to gain their support. We also look at the importance of being data-driven and the diversity data you should collect. Finally, we consider how getting recognized for EDI efforts can help to attract diverse talent and support your business case.

LEARNING OBJECTIVES

By the end of this chapter, you will be able to:

- Assess perceptions of EDI and their impact.
- Understand how to navigate pushback against EDI and the things to be clear on to gain support for initiatives.
- Secure senior leadership buy-in by aligning metrics and soft power with organizational strategy and building a business case.
- Understand the benefits to the organization of seeking recognition and accreditation for EDI efforts.

Navigating pushback

Society and organizations face changes and challenges on every front: whether domestically like the cost-of-living crisis, unemployment, homelessness, strike action, public sector services and cuts to funding, Brexit, immigration and skills gaps, or globally like political instability, wars, populism, refugees, trade tariffs, climate change, inflation, ageing populations, cybercrime, AI and working from home. A number of these issues directly relate to EDI, some presenting opportunities, but others posing a threat.

EDI is sometimes brought into the spotlight for all the wrong reasons, and it can move up and down an organization's priority list depending on social and political shifts. As an EDI practitioner, it's sometimes necessary to push harder for EDI initiatives, during times when the concept is not viewed as a priority by leadership.

For example, in 2023, the clothing store ASOS opted to scrap EDI targets and in 2024, the UK government announced the end of civil service spending on EDI, suggesting that current EDI roles would be consolidated into existing HR teams and there would be no more new hires dedicated solely to EDI. These are just two examples that are suggestive of a worrying downward trend, giving the message that EDI work is less of a priority. If you are a minority, this shift is likely to marginalize you further.

Why is this shift happening? In Chapter 1, we considered cases such as the Gender Pay Gap, the #MeToo and #BLM movements, the murder of George Floyd and Sarah Everard. These resulted in a targeted focus on misogyny and racism, and more broadly diversity, and EDI moved up the priority list for many organizations. This led to a plethora of EDI roles being created and filled, often seeing appointees who lacked experience being funded to carry out quick-fix EDI initiatives. The aim was normally to be seen to be doing something, but people often didn't think about what they wanted to measure.

Some EDI initiatives materialize as big, (expensive) showpieces without any real sustainable impact, giving EDI a bad reputation and raising questions over the value to the organization. The issue is, some are often stand-alone and detached from the core services being delivered or done as an afterthought.

Many of these initiatives focus on attracting diverse talent, creating awareness and understanding, whether through parades or fireside chats. However, they do not go the extra mile to appreciate the lived experience, thereby failing to create cultures of inclusion, where diversity feels it belongs.

This meant the return on investment was missing for senior leaders, who, after investing, could not see the value for money; how it impacted retention or better served their customers or service users. Consequently, the pendulum has swung the other way, and EDI has fallen down the priority list, paying the price of a lack of foresight.

What can we do?

HR needs to assess the employee lifecycle outlined in Chapters 6 and 7 as a whole and work strategically, thinking long-term, not short-term, to remove barriers and create more equity from the point of recruitment and selection to termination. Initiatives must be clear about the following:

- What they aim to achieve.
- Why it is important.
- How long it will take.
- The required costs and resources.
- The difference it will make to the business.
- The measures of success.

These would be reasonable questions to address for any business commitment as part of the decision-making process. There is a real danger of organizations, 'throwing out the baby with the bath water', because an EDI initiative hasn't delivered tangible results.

> **STOP AND THINK**
>
> What is the current feeling towards EDI in your organization? Have you noticed a shift in priority up or down the agenda?

Getting buy-in from senior leaders

If you're working in EDI, you are not going to be successful working alone. You will need 'buy-in' from your line manager and senior leaders from across the organization. One of the common pitfalls for any HR initiative, including EDI, is getting 'buy-in' from senior leaders.

HR can be regarded as neither strategic nor aligned with business objectives. This can be because an HR project has not been well articulated or planned properly and is instead a mere response to what is currently popular or trending within the profession.

Too often, EDI initiatives are not a response to the actual 'pain points' of the organization. To put it another way, they don't answer the questions that keep leaders up at night, such as:

- Is the organization growing, and what needs to be done to contribute to organizational growth?
- Does the organization have international aspirations?
- Is the organization driven by quality or low-cost differentiation in delivering its products and services?
- Is the organization downsizing?
- Is the organization relocating?

How could these questions relate to EDI strategy? Can EDI help to answer them? Or is EDI a standalone function, disparate from the vision and mission of the organization? Let's take the first question as an example – 'Is the organization growing, and what needs to be done to contribute to organizational growth?' Most organizations have growth aspirations, and to grow, they need the right talent. In Chapter 6, we explored how having diverse talent puts organizations at a competitive advantage. Diversity brings innovation and different perspectives. So, if the challenge is recruiting the right talent, how can we change the way we think about talent to address it?

Once you have clarified what the pain points are, what you need is a business case.

The EDI business case

A business case puts your proposal into a language the business can understand. For ease, we'll outline the thinking by looking at a very basic example of an HR initiative to boost wellbeing and reduce absence rates – introducing 'Fresh Fruit Friday' or a gym membership for everyone. In principle, it sounds great, but there needs to be a basis for the initiative and clarity on the outcomes expected to demonstrate a return on investment. Or simply put, why should the organization spend X amount of money?

Robust business cases must address certain questions. Say 'Fresh Fruit Friday' or gym membership has been running for a few months as part of a trial, and you are writing a business case to make it permanent. For business leaders to make a decision, they will need to know the following:

- What were the sickness absence rates before 'Fresh Fruit Fridays' or the start of gym membership?
- How does this compare with similar-sized organizations in the same industry sector?
- How does this compare to previous years?
- Are there any peaks and troughs?
- What has already been tried?
- How long will 'Fresh Fruit Fridays' or gym membership run for? A month, three months, a year?
- What will it cost?
- What has been the uptake?
- What were the sickness absence rates after 'Fresh Fruit Fridays' or gym memberships started?
- What was the anecdotal feedback?
- When will a review take place?

Being ready to answer these questions increases the likelihood of funding and approval from senior leaders and explores whether or not fresh fruit or gym membership is the right thing to do. There needs to be clarity on the problem you are trying to solve, or the opportunity you are trying to take advantage of.

This approach can be adopted for any EDI initiative, allowing you to demonstrate added value and positioning yourself as a serious professional. It also aligns with the CIPD's Profession Map, which the organization describes as 'the international standard for the people profession'. It describes the core values, knowledge, behaviours and specialist knowledge necessary to be an effective HR professional. The values it lists are: 'principles-led', 'evidence-based' and 'outcomes-driven'. Creating an organization where everyone has value and is afforded their dignity is very much about being principles-led, while also being evidence-based. Outcomes are all about quantitative and qualitative data, which takes us nicely into the importance of metrics.

EXERCISE

Think of a current EDI initiative you are working on. Can you adapt the questions listed above for this initiative and answer them?

Metrics matter

You might have come into the HR profession to work with people, but numbers can't be escaped.

EXPERT OPINION

Jonathan Ferrar, CEO of Insight 222 and co-author of *Excellence in People Analytics*

When it comes to EDI, there are many ways to think about data and insights. Firstly, at the most basic level, it is knowing which categories of represented groups are in the employee population. Then it is about reporting on issues that are required to meet compliance and regulatory standards. However, at a much more advanced level, it is about using data to help the organization evolve and iterate to be more inclusive.

When it comes to any piece of work, including EDI, metrics are the starting point. To address some of the issues raised in this book, the importance of being data-driven cannot be stressed enough.

Knowing who you have employed is the basis of everything else that follows when trying to create an inclusive workplace, but capturing diversity data can be the first stumbling block in this area of work. Knowing how many people are in your organization is the starting point. If you don't know this, by default, you don't know how many are male, female, Black, white, disabled or their age etc. The phrase, 'What gets measured, gets managed', attributed (falsely) to management guru Peter Drucker, comes to mind. If you don't know where you are currently in terms of diversity, how do you then measure and report on progress?

Capturing personal demographics data and reporting on it sends a clear message: the organization is not oblivious to who you are and what your needs are. Failing to do it robustly, or at all, can send a very negative message and harm your employer brand.

Capturing demographic data is often done at the application stage, when candidates are asked to fill in an Equal Opportunities Questionnaire or Diversity Monitoring Form with questions focused on protected characteristics, but also other areas like social mobility, political activity or spent criminal convictions.

Typically, there will be clarification that this information is purely for capturing diversity data, which will be anonymized and is not part of the selection and recruitment process. Therefore, it is not seen at the shortlisting stage or later by the interview panel.

Some of the data disclosed can be more obvious once the person has been appointed, such as gender, ethnicity or age, so disclosure of this information is usually complete.

However, other personal information, such as that related to non-visible disability or sexual orientation, is not always as freely disclosed by candidates, out of fear of stigma and antici-pated discrimination, with candidates opting for 'prefer not to say'. This option is helpful insofar as no one should feel compelled to disclose personal information they are uncomfortable with, but it can also mean data is skewed.

Collecting personal demographic data is not limited to the application stage, and especially for longer-serving staff, may not be retained or relevant due to changed circumstances. Getting this information very much depends on an employer's track record with their work, or lack of it, on EDI. If employees have concerns about sharing personal data with their employer and how it will be stored and protected, they will not give much away. If these concerns exist within the organization, it is important to address them, because capturing diversity data is foundational to EDI work and becomes the foundation of everything that follows.

What data should you collect?

Examples of foundational diversity data you should aim to collect:

- **Talent attraction:** How many applications received are from diverse, marginalized groups? Of these, how many progress to the interview stage? And of these, how many are successfully appointed?
- **Retention:** How many people from diverse, marginalized groups are still with the organization, and how does this compare to the wider population?
- **Training and development:** How many people from diverse, marginalized groups started training? How many completed training successfully? What were the benefits to them and the organization?
- **Wellbeing:** Do any marginalized groups have higher sickness absence than others?
  - This question is true for all other HR areas of concern, such as performance management, disciplinaries, grievances and dismissals, such as redundancies.

> **TOP TIP**
> Recognize the importance of data
>
> You might be tempted to skip data collection, as it can be hard, but remember what the late American economist William Deming is purported to have said, 'Without data, you are just another person with an opinion'.

Using soft power

> **Soft power:** Soft power is the ability to influence others and shape outcomes through attraction, persuasion and cultural appeal rather than force or relying on formal authority.

As we noted in Chapter 2, where EDI sits in an organization can vary. This book has been written with early career HR professionals in mind. You are therefore unlikely to report directly to the CEO or the HR director. If you did, it would be relatively easy to gain support for your efforts to bring about positive change. Once you had those one or two individuals on side, you'd have a reasonable amount of hierarchical power yourself.

As an early career professional, you are unlikely to have this visibility and reach in the hierarchy. So what can you do? Use your soft power. Tap into your own power of communication, as referred to in Chapter 2. Find allies, those aligned with the principles of EDI and with hierarchical power. Through their advocacy and support, your role in delivering EDI can attain more buy-in from senior leaders. Your ability to connect with others effectively becomes a critical deciding factor in how successful you are likely to be.

In 1959, social psychologists John R. P. French and Bertram Raven suggested that there are five 'bases of power': coercive, reward, legitimate, referent and expert.[1] They further suggested that to get buy-in and be persuasive in presenting ideas, you should lean into two of these types: expert and referent.

- Expert power means being able to demonstrate a high level of skill and knowledge in your subject area, which the first half of this book will be able to help you with.
- Referent power is concerned with your perceived attractiveness, worthiness and right to others' respect. So, being authentic, transparent, open and generally 'nice' will enable others to connect with you more deeply.

TOP TIP
Use your soft power to get support for your business case

Soft power allows your voice, visibility and reach to be amplified, enabling support for your EDI business case.

Recognition

Many employers seek accreditation, sign up to charters and submit for an EDI award, which they then display on their websites, marketing materials and recruitment campaigns.

While most organizations claim to be equal opportunity employers, getting some form of validation certainly helps with attracting diverse talent and goes some way towards creating an inclusive culture.

KEY POINT

While badging is not required, it does send a positive statement of intent, especially when recognized by an external body. This can support your business case, as most employers welcome positive publicity associated with their brand.

Standards and charters

- National Equality Standard: provides clear criteria against which companies can assess their EDI policies and practices.
- Investors in People: An international standard committed to effective people management, fostering inclusive workplace cultures, and promoting employee development.
- Athena Swan Charter: Recognizes commitment to gender equality in the advancement and promotion of staff and students in higher education and research.
- Race at Work Charter: An initiative by Business in the Community, outlining actions for employers to improve racial equality and inclusion in the workplace.
- Disability Confident: A UK government scheme, encouraging employers to recruit and retain disabled people, recognizing those who create inclusive work environments.
- Faith at Work: Programmes or policies supporting religious diversity in the workplace, ensuring employees can practice their faith without discrimination.
- Stonewall: A UK-based LGBTQ+ rights organization, advocating for equality and offering diversity training to promote inclusive workplaces.
- Armed Forces Covenant: A pledge by organizations to support veterans, ensuring they are treated fairly in society and the workplace.

Lists of best organizations

There are various lists celebrating organizations committed to and excelling in EDI practices.

- 'Top Workplaces' DE&I Practices Award', based on employee feedback and organizational policies.
- 'Best Companies Group's Inclusive Workplace Recognition' is determined by comprehensive employee surveys.

- 'Inclusive Top 50 UK Employers', awarded by Inclusive Companies judged by EDI experts based on an entry submission.

Awards

Awards nights are typically glitzy events and can be a great way to celebrate success. Awards are judged by peers, with organizations often making multiple written submissions to several awarding bodies.

Being shortlisted, highly commended or winning the top prize on the night is highly sought after and helps to visibly position EDI within organizations.

Some of the more well-known awards hosted by the HR industry include:

- CIPD People Management: Best EDI Initiative.
- HR Excellence: Best D&I Strategy.
- Culture Pioneer: Inclusion Award
- Business Culture: Best DEI Initiative.
- Personnel Today: EDI Award.

There are other awards, such as the British Diversity Awards, Inclusive Awards and the National Diversity Awards.

If you have developed a good business case and implemented EDI successfully, then all the ingredients of an award submission are to hand if you can clarify why, what, how, outcomes, and impact.

The risk with awards is that they are mostly judged according to the written submissions and supporting documentation, which are not always reflective of the reality internally, so there is a risk of cognitive dissonance.

TOP TIP
Find out what staff think of your efforts

To find out what staff think of your EDI efforts, look on Glassdoor. The website includes a D&I rating based on staff feedback.

WHAT WOULD YOU DO?
Number 8

An applicant has contacted HR to complain that when asked to complete the data monitoring form, they did not have the option to select their faith, Islam, but other world faiths were listed, including smaller religious followings.

- What are the concerns with this process?
- What can HR do to address this issue?

CHAPTER SUMMARY

- EDI goes through 'boom and bust' periods, where it is seen as more and less of a priority in society and organizations.
- Having a good business case underpinned by metrics can help win support for EDI.
- Use your soft power to find allies and influence senior leadership.
- Achieving external recognition for your EDI efforts can help attract diverse talent and support your employer brand.

REVIEW QUESTIONS

1 Why does EDI move up and down priority lists?

2 Why is it important to be clear on the 'why' behind EDI initiatives?

3 List three typical business questions a senior leader would want an EDI initiative to address.

Endnote

1   http://www.communicationcache.com/uploads/1/0/8/8/10887248/the_bases_ of_social_power_-_chapter_20_-_1959.pdf (archived at https://perma.cc/ BB54-HB4C)

Conclusion

This book has sought to introduce you to the evolving world of EDI. Too often, EDI has been reduced to a training programme or celebration event, but as you now know, it is so much more than that. EDI is an area that has been around in some shape or form since the 1900s, with various focuses at different points in time, and continues to evolve through legislation, tribunal cases, research and societal influences. Carrying the mantle to deliver EDI interventions means that you, too, need to evolve. EDI has not stood still, so neither can you.

This Conclusion provides further guidance on developing your skills, knowledge, competencies and behaviours to support future activities in this critical area of HR work, which impacts the employee lifecycle, products and services. As you work through it, reflect on your current skills and understanding of EDI, bearing in mind your own organization's attitude towards it, its maturity and your desired future career direction.

This book may be coming to an end, but your journey has only just begun.

LEARNING OBJECTIVES

By the end of this chapter, you will be able to:

- Reinforce your understanding of the key takeaways from previous chapters.

- Identify areas for future learning.
- Reflect on your skills in the area of EDI.
- Develop an action plan for effective EDI development.

Summary of key takeaways

- EDI starts with understanding Equality, Equity, Diversity and Inclusion and how they interconnect.
- The world of work was not designed for difference, leading to demographic disparities in the workforce. Addressing these disparities could help win the 'war for talent'.
- Organizational values can support alignment with EDI principles.
- EDI is an essential part of HR models, featuring at every stage of the employee lifecycle.
- Familiarity with EDI terminology is highly beneficial and useful.
- Qualification in EDI can significantly help to increase credibility.
- Soft skills can help to connect, communicate and advocate for EDI.
- Equality legislation means protected characteristics are equal, but world events result in some being more equal than others.
- Everyone has multiple biases which particularly surface when using System 1 thinking.
- We all have an irrational fear of difference, which can result in the stereotyping of marginalized groups.
- Several psychology studies help us understand how difference, exclusion and power imbalance surface in the workplace.
- Common EDI initiatives are used across sectors to create inclusive cultures, but they vary in resources, commitment and impact.

- Greater attention needs to be placed on the employee life-cycle, with a focus on how to attract, develop, reward and retain diverse talent. To access talent more widely, it must be redefined.
- It is critical to familiarize ourselves with types of discrimination, harassment and bullying and to ensure equitable resolutions.
- EDI can go through 'boom and bust' periods, in line with political and social shifts.

Your ongoing development in EDI

The world of EDI is continuously evolving, so to remain relevant and effective, prioritize your continuous personal development.

- While key terminology, outlined in Chapter 1, has not significantly changed, it is important to understand the nuances, interrelationships and dependencies to ensure credibility.
- Review all the EDI terms in Chapter 2, as well as reading other definitions and explanations, so that you are fluent enough to engage with the terms confidently. (But remember not to hide behind them!)
- Keep informed about any research that evidences how EDI is good for business, particularly in terms of revenue growth and impact on wellbeing.
- Follow global news, events and legislation, taking note of any societal shifts and movements that may be relevant to marginalized groups.
- If you have your own lived experience and related trauma, address it through counselling. From a wellbeing perspective, you must prioritize your own needs to help others.
- Assess whether you have the right qualifications to be competent and credible in this discipline. If not, consider your qualification options.

- Attend EDI conferences and events to hear from industry specialists and learn about the latest thinking and case studies.
- Consider finding EDI mentors, both inside and outside of your sector – someone to discuss your ideas with, who can guide and challenge your thinking. Nurture this network of EDI connections by following them on LinkedIn, reading their posts and, if possible, meeting them for coffee to pick their brains.
- Read HR publications like *HR Magazine, Personnel Today, HR Zone, HR Grapevine, People Space, HR Director* and CIPD's *People Management Awards.* These publications feature interviews, articles and case studies on best practices, but remember that best practice doesn't always mean best fit.

Performing a self-assessment

In this section, we'll recap the skills you need to be an effective EDI practitioner. You are also encouraged to revisit bias, which we covered in detail in Chapter 3.

Skills

Chapter 2 outlined the skills essential for an effective EDI practitioner, as listed below:

- Mindset.
- Empathy.
- Curiosity.
- Cultural competency.
- Self-awareness.
- Numeracy.
- Communication.

Score yourself out of 10 on each skill to identify your strengths and weaknesses. Ask someone who knows you well to score you too, to uncover any 'blind spots'.

Play to your strengths. Reflect on your low scores and set realistic goals for improvement. Understand that it's not about eliminating a low score but rather it's about being aware of the issue and mitigating it through learning, practice and support.

Bias

Are you clear on your own bias and what drives your behaviour? Sometimes you need to get out of your own way to be effective. We are all flawed, as explained in Chapters 3 and 4. That's part of what makes us human, but there are steps we can take to become even better humans.

EXPERT OPINION

Stephen Frost, CEO of Included and author of *The Key to Inclusion*

To expose your bias and consider your racism, ask yourself these four simple questions:

- Consider your partner or spouse, now or previously. Are they from the same ethnic background as you?
- Consider your best friend or group of friends. Are they from the same ethnic background as you?
- Consider your neighbours where you live. Are they from the same ethnic background as you?
- Consider a social activity or hobby you do with others. Are they from the same ethnic background as you?

If you answered yes to any of these questions, does that make you a racist? Not necessarily, but it does mean that race has probably influenced your thinking to some degree, resulting in affinity bias. This might also apply across a number of areas, not limited to one difference.

We choose who to spend time with, but the world of work has the power to bring together all kinds of different people. Having positive interactions with those we perceive as different helps to break down barriers, resists an 'us versus them' mindset, and frees us from our own echo chambers.

> **TOP TIP**
>
> Seek out those who are different from you. Getting to know people who are different from you helps you to see the person, not the difference.

Action planning your EDI strategy

It is crucial to be clear about the problem you are trying to solve. The EDI strategy cannot be based on what others are doing, as it must be relevant to *your* organization's needs. It should be evidence-based and aligned with the organizational strategy.

If EDI initiatives do not resonate with your organization's aims, you will face an uphill struggle and budgetary constraints. Demanding that everyone 'get on board or get out of the way' is ill-advised. It is better to take people with you on the journey.

Like with any strategy, it's vital to understand where the organization currently stands with regard to EDI, where it needs to be, and what actions are required to get there.

An equity audit, contracted to an external EDI consultancy collating both quantitative and qualitative data, can fast-track the answer to the organization's current state, but is a more costly option. In any case, it is important to accept that whatever the issues are, it is unlikely you will fix them all; rather it is about moving the dial in the right direction. It certainly will not be overnight. Instead, making real, holistic change will take time and involve taking 'baby steps' until you have earned the trust and support of senior leaders. Take a long-term view. After all, Rome was not built in a day. The following are all possible actions to consider:

- Learn about your sector to identify the demographic challenges that need addressing. Understand your customers or service users. Who are you delivering products and services to? Is this demographic reflected in your organization? This will require capturing demographic personal information, if it has not been collated already.
- Speak to hiring managers and HR recruitment advisers to understand the skills gap in the workforce and identify the hard-to-fill roles. Discuss whether these can be addressed by thinking about talent differently.
- Review your current organizational values to see if any support EDI and can bolster support for the work you're doing.
- Assess whether organizational policies are inclusive, particularly those in the employee handbook. Meet with policy owners and review the policy together through an EDI lens. Assess whether they currently support and value difference.
- Identify metrics that would be helpful to collate and assess whether the team has the capacity and capability to do so. Consider whether current HR metrics provide any insights into disproportionate and inequitable treatment towards marginalized groups.
- Review any EDI-related questions and responses on the staff survey to see if there are useful insights into how marginalized groups are feeling to establish a benchmark. Assess whether the response rate is sufficiently representative of the workforce. If not, this may expose an issue with psychological safety and a lack of trust in the leadership. If there isn't currently a staff survey, initiate one with relevant EDI questions around belonging (see Chapter 1).
- Map out diversity in the organization, making note of any 'glass ceilings' in leadership roles. Consider organizing a listening session with the workforce to understand what barriers may exist and whether interventions like coaching or mentoring could make a difference.

- Understand the gender pay gap. Find out what has already been done to address it and assess what else could be done. Consider voluntarily disclosing other pay gaps to bring a focus on a specific area of difference.
- Identify allies in the organization, (preferably in influential roles), who can advocate for your work. This may be your line manager, but not necessarily. Meet with the individual to share your ideas, seeking their support and buy-in for EDI.
- Create safe spaces, whether for prayer and self-reflection, or platforms such as employee resource groups if they do not already exist.
- Ensure employee resource groups have clear terms of reference and are adequately resourced. Encourage employee resource groups to share learnings with one another.
- Take a joined-up approach (see worked example), rather than treating each initiative as stand alone, also considering intersectionality.
- Present your findings to the decision makers in a way that avoids jargon and delivers key messages, to garner support for the work you have planned.
- Book a one-to-one meeting with your line manager to discuss your own development and ongoing support.

Whatever actions are decided on can be detailed in an action plan – an example of a worked example is given in Table 9.1.

Final thoughts

EDI is more important than ever, and you are a part of this movement. You can contribute to creating a more inclusive and diverse environment, making the workplace a safe place for everyone. This book will serve as a guide to help you do just that. So, what are you waiting for? EDI is an exciting place to be – go change the world.

TABLE 9.1 A worked example of an action plan for EDI strategy

What	Why (evidence-based)	How	Cost	Outputs	Impact (outcome driven)
Mentoring programme for a specific marginalized group.	Staff survey findings (quantitative) and listening groups (qualitative) have identified barriers to promotion.	Managers supported and trained. Time protected.	£10,000.	20 mentees.	4 senior appointments.

Answers to 'What would you do?' exercises

This appendix gives suggested responses to the 'What would you do?' exercises included throughout this book. These exercises are designed to help you apply concepts in real-world scenarios and reflect on how you might approach practical challenges in a thoughtful, informed way.

Each answer highlights the issues at stake and offers an example of how a situation could be handled. They are not definitive solutions, but rather indicative responses meant to stimulate critical thinking and help you explore possible approaches.

You may find that your responses differ from the following; that's completely normal. Check out what's different and identify any gaps in knowledge.

WHAT WOULD YOU DO? NUMBER 1

The issues
While the recruiting manager believes they are being fair by treating everyone 'the same', they have not considered equity, recognizing that barriers may exist which need to be removed so every applicant has a fair opportunity. If applicants are being excluded based on cultural fit, it suggests that the recruiting manager does not want difference in their team, which could be

discriminatory, breaching the Equality 2010 and missing out on a great candidate.

The solution

Explain the difference between equity and equality to the recruiting manager and ask them to consider 'cultural add' rather than 'cultural fit', pointing out that applicants who are different may bring unique perspectives or strengths to the team.

It may be helpful to remind the recruiting manager about the Equality Act 2010 and the nine protected characteristics to ensure the organization is not being put at risk of legal action.

WHAT WOULD YOU DO? NUMBER 2

The issues

Having diverse views in the workplace is unavoidable, given everyone will have different lived experiences. However, these views should be aired respectfully and in the right way. There is a risk of undermining EDI efforts and creating division in the organization, potentially leading to disciplinary actions depending on the views being expressed, especially if they are discriminatory.

The solution

The employee could be made aware of the potential impact their views could have on others, unintentionally causing harm and distress to marginalized groups.

Stressing to the employee that being inclusive is aligned with the organization's values, where applicable, would help to underscore the need for EDI training.

EDI training, ironically, is probably what would help this employee. EDI training often involves creating safe spaces to challenge preconceptions about EDI, to support the employee's learning so they can be more self-aware and open to those we perceive as different. Learning does not end with just EDI training, but can be the starting point for inclusive conversations to ensure better understanding.

WHAT WOULD YOU DO? NUMBER 3

The issues
The manager has discounted Ayesha without giving her a fair opportunity to progress her career. It is likely that the manager has opted not to give Ayesha projects or responsibilities where she can demonstrate her leadership capability.

The manager's view may be biased and exacerbated by a negative stereotype rooted in System 1 thinking as well as a lack of understanding around different cultures and neurodivergence.

The solution
Challenge the manager on her assumptions by asking, 'What evidence are your views based on?' Ask the manager to share specific examples of behaviours or performance that concern her.

You could also propose that the manager give Ayesha some pieces of work to stretch and develop her. This would enable the manager to assess her readiness for bigger pieces of work and leadership responsibility. Stress to the manager that she needs to provide support to Ayesha to set her up to succeed. She might also like to consider a coach to help develop her confidence.

It may be helpful for the manager to speak to other peers and team members who have worked with Ayesha, to arrive at a more holistic viewpoint of Ayesha's potential.

Finally, the manager may benefit from training on understanding differences related to faith practices and neurodiversity.

WHAT WOULD YOU DO? NUMBER 4

The issues
The sales teams' views are likely to translate into bullying behaviours and possibly discrimination, given the different ethnic make-up of the two teams. This toxic culture is not likely to be conducive to collaborative working, thereby impacting the organization. If left unchallenged, there is a likelihood that

members of the logistics and transportation team will have higher levels of sickness absence, grievances and staff turnover, impacting the whole organization.

The solution

The importance of mutual respect and the impact of behaviours need to be stressed to both the sales team and the logistics and transportation team. Senior leaders in both teams need to role model the behaviours expected from the teams they are leading.

Sales team members could spend more time with their colleagues in the logistics and transportation team to break down artificial barriers and perceptions about 'the other'. This could be done through formal interventions like shadowing or informal routes such as away days and mixing up the teams to work on small projects.

More broadly, each part of the organization needs to understand the importance and relevance of every part of the organization, on the basis that 'the whole is more than the sum of the parts', attributed to Aristotle.

WHAT WOULD YOU DO? NUMBER 5

The issues

It is not clear how the competitors' EDI initiatives translated into what is being reported. There is no obvious correlation between the use of enforced pronouns and a 20 per cent increase in gender balance. It is more likely that the mentoring has resulted in a specific gender continuing in the organization to pursue opportunities, which has reduced attrition rates.

Also, what does 20 per cent mean, quantifiably? If there was one female and now there are two, that would be a 100 per cent increase. But without knowing the size of the organization, it's hard to say how significant an achievement it is.

Finally, 'cutting and pasting' what someone else has done in their organization will not necessarily result in the same outcomes in yours, as 'best practice' does not necessarily mean 'best fit'.

The solution

Discuss with your boss what problem needs to be addressed. Understand whether there is an issue with attracting and retaining a certain gender. This requires an analysis of the current gender balance and how it compares across the industry and hierarchy. For example, in the HR profession, females make up 90 per cent of junior roles, 60 per cent of overall roles, but only 39 per cent of leadership roles.

Consider benchmark data from others in your industry to see how you compare.

Advise your boss that mentoring alone would not necessarily address gender imbalance. Instead, a range of coordinated EDI initiatives is likely to be needed.

Review attraction and staff turnover by gender to understand if any underlying issues need a different solution tailored to your specific needs.

WHAT WOULD YOU DO? NUMBER 6

The issues

John may well be the best person for the role, but how would Kevin know this if Ayotunde and others have not had a fair and equal opportunity to apply for the role? Kevin appears to have an affinity bias towards John, possibly linked to race, gender and age.

The lack of any process involved in the appointment exposes the organization to potential discrimination claims if Ayotunde feels excluded because of her protected characteristics of race, gender and/or age, which will be difficult to defend as the decision is not grounded in core competencies needed for the role.

The impact of appointments without a process sends a wider message to all staff that progression is dependent on personal relationships or nepotism rather than merit, so it will lead to talented staff looking outside of the organization to develop their careers.

The solution

Kevin was able to appoint without any process, suggesting this is an organization-wide issue that needs to be addressed immediately. Meet with all recruiting managers and explain the value of having diverse recruitment panels using competency-based questions aligned with the needs of the role.

Arrange training for all recruitment managers to cover the Equality Act 2010, unconscious bias and how to use a competency framework to appoint the best candidates rather than a 'culture fit'.

The post needs to be re-advertised internally, with John advised that he can apply alongside other internal applicants. In this specific instance, it may be necessary for Kevin to be removed from the recruitment process as there appears to be a conflict of interest or at least not be able to score John's application and interview.

Blind CVs are not likely to work in this recruitment as it is internal, and candidates are likely to be identifiable.

WHAT WOULD YOU DO? NUMBER 7

The issues

Being excluded and not being heard is a type of microaggression. Saoirse is also being gaslit and clearly lacks confidence that her concerns are going to be addressed. Her resignation is a possible sign of 'learned helplessness' and adds to staff attrition while allowing the negative behaviours to go unchallenged.

The solution

Meet with Saoirse off-site or in a safe place to probe further into her reasons for leaving.

The managers need training to ensure they are inclusive, as well as the importance of managing feedback and concerns from direct reports.

Channels for reporting concerns need to be introduced and communicated to all staff so that there is always a route and safe space for remedial action to be taken to address issues in real time.

'Stay' interviews could be introduced, which are similar to exit interviews in understanding why a staff member may be thinking of leaving before it happens, by which point it is too late.

WHAT WOULD YOU DO? NUMBER 8

The issues

Omitting a faith followed by almost 1.8 billion people potentially sent a very negative message to every Muslim applicant: 'Your faith doesn't matter, we don't see you, and this is not important to us as an organization'. The likelihood is that a good number of any organization's customers or service users would be from that demographic group, who could feel alienated if this were to become public knowledge.

The solution

Review what data is being collected to identify any gaps in collation because this data will be critical to measure the impact of all your EDI initiatives.

While there is no definitive list, it is important to include some of the nine protected characteristics. Others could include socioeconomic background, right to work and criminal convictions. However, applicants must be able to select the option 'Prefer not to say', as participation must be voluntary.

Looking for another book?

Explore our award-winning books from global business experts in Human Resources, Learning and Development

Scan the code to browse

www.koganpage.com/hr-learning-development

Our Brand New HR Skills Series

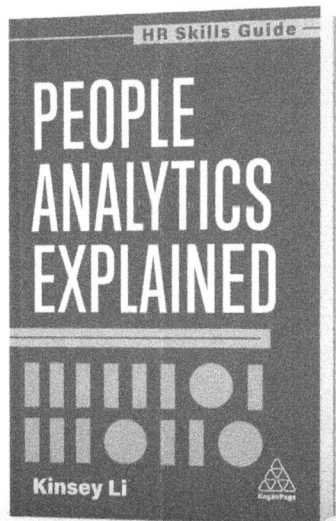

All the knowledge and skills for your HR Career

KoganPage

From 4 December 2025 the EU Responsible Person (GPSR) is:
eucomply oÜ, Pärnu mnt. 139b – 14, 11317 Tallinn, Estonia
www.eucompliancepartner.com

www.ingramcontent.com/pod-product-compliance
Lightning Source LLC
Chambersburg PA
CBHW061024220326
41597CB00019BB/3318